Dedicated to all those facing the daily challenge of diabetes and to the many others committed to conquering this pervasive disease

Contents

Foreword

Nicole Johnson
Miss America 1999

Healthy eating is imperative for someone with diabetes. There are a bevy of food choices out there, but where do you start and what is a busy person to do? This book is the answer to those questions!

When Mr. Food and I first met, I went on and on about how frustrating it is for me to make great-tasting, quick meals that would fit into my diabetes meal plan. It was then that the idea for this book was born. Consequently, Mr. Food and I have teamed up to bring you some of the best diabetic recipes available, of course, in his signature quick-and-easy fashion.

During my reign as Miss America 1999, I had the opportunity to spread the word throughout the world about what diabetes is and how to seek help for its diagnosis, treatment, and prevention. What a pleasure and honor it has been to share my experiences with so many. However, it has also been the biggest challenge of my life. Today I continue to travel worldwide, and I have visited many countries in the name of diabetes awareness and education. Truthfully, that is the other reason I collaborated on this book. We need to continuously seek new venues in which to exchange information and, in turn, educate the public about this critical illness.

Diabetes is pervasive, dangerous, and at times devastating. However, with careful maintenance, specifically a proper diet, many of its complications can be prevented or at least delayed. Those complications range from heart disease to stroke, blindness, and even kidney failure. Someday we will find a cure for this disease, but until that day, this book is intended to serve as a tool in our daily care. Our practice of the principles within, as people with diabetes, exemplifies our combined commitment to better health.

One of the biggest obstacles in daily care is finding the time to eat right. How does the busy professional or the hurried parent prepare foods that are tempting to the eye and the palate? Mr. Food has continued to do what he does so well by coming up with recipes that are quick, easy, and prepared with readily available ingredients. For a person like me—like most of us—this combination is a blessing!

Beyond food preparation, issues such as portion size and label reading are also key elements for the person living with diabetes or the person preparing his or her meals. These issues are addressed here, too.

I charge you to do what you can to control your diabetes for life. It won't be easy. At times you may want to throw in the towel, but realize that in adversity our souls are strengthened, our vision is cleared, our ambition is inspired, and success is achieved. I believe that anything is possible—including a life free of complications from diabetes. And remember, any time you need quick information or a boost of encouragement, visit my website, *www.nicolejohnson.com*; you can even send me an e-mail from there.

Enjoy this helpful tool! I pray that you are blessed by the information included and that, from it, your diabetes management becomes a little quicker and easier.

Nicole Johnson

Nicole Johnson
Miss America 1999, Author and Diabetes Advocate

Preface

Art Ginsburg
Mr. Food

When the original edition of this book was published in 2001, I couldn't have known the impact it would have. I had received so many requests for recipes that would fit into diabetes meal plans that, when this book finally came out, it practically became a food bible for many of those with diabetes.

With the ADA's extensive diabetes resources, Nicole Johnson's first-hand experiences, and my no-nonsense quick approach to cooking, we created a winning "I can do it!" book that is truly useful for people with diabetes.

And now that the ADA has revised their nutritional guidelines and brought them in line with other low-fat, heart-healthy meal plans, we decided to revise these recipes and publish a second edition. If it means better helping people living with diabetes, I'm all for it!

As with my earlier edition, these recipes will add excitement to a diabetic meal plan—so you don't have to suffer with the "same old, same old" boring diabetic recipes. You can enjoy dishes that are tasty and, of course, quick, too.

The over 150 no-nonsense recipes in this book were each tested, tasted, and retested until I was personally satisfied. When I serve these to others and the response is, "This is for a diabetic cookbook? No way! It's so good!" or "I thought people with diabetes couldn't eat dessert!" that's when I know I've got a winner.

I've learned so much about diabetes since starting work on this book. What amazes me the most, and what's gonna make you really happy, is that you, a person with diabetes, can eat most of the foods you love! The diabetic meal plan isn't just centering on salads and plain foods anymore; now it features mouth-watering dishes and even delectable desserts. Where's the catch? Moderation—in the way you prepare your meals and in your portion sizes. Get used to the word moderation, 'cause it's vital to a healthy lifestyle, and you'll be seeing it over and over throughout this book.

The key to eating well really starts at the supermarket with reading labels. On page 3, I explain what all those numbers mean on nutrition labels. And, after making your food choices, remember to focus on portion control. My "Portion Pointers" on page 8 will fill you in (not up)! When planning your meals and snacks with your registered dietitian, ask how you can work in portions of your favorite foods or special desserts. Your dietitian can show you how to make adjustments in other parts of your meal plan or change your exercise schedule.

I don't want you to think that this book will answer all your questions about what you can eat, but my recipes sure can make mealtime a lot easier and more enjoyable. Plus, I've sprinkled it liberally with tips on everything from adding pizzazz to your meals to caring for your body. For more great recipe ideas and food tips, be sure to check my website, *www.mrfood.com*.

With all this helpful information and these tasty recipes, you should be able to gain control over what and how you are eating. Beyond that, you also need to exercise! Just because you eat correctly doesn't mean you can skip regular exercise.

Developing good eating habits and changing your lifestyle may take a little time. Be patient, and don't leave it all behind when you eat out! Again, check "Portion Pointers" (page 8) for some sensible suggestions, continue to think "moderation," and you should be fine.

I know you are going to be surprised with what's in here – and with it all, you'll be able to surprise your gang, too. Make these recipes your own. As always, if you have any questions about your individual meal plan, contact your physician or dietitian.

Whether you're making these good-for-us recipes for yourself or someone else, cooking is the best way to share our love, and that's the true meaning of . . .

"OOH IT'S SO GOOD!!®"

Acknowledgments

Wow! I said that in the first edition of this book, and I have to say it again: The response the American Diabetes Association, Nicole Johnson, and I have gotten to this book has been just incredible. And I have so many people to thank for its success.

First, there's Nicole Johnson. The idea for this book started with our chance meeting during Nicole's reign as Miss America 1999. I had been receiving requests for recipes for people with diabetes, so when Nicole told me about the personal challenges diabetes had presented to her, we knew we could make a difference together. We were determined to create tasty, quick dishes that she—and really everyone with diabetes—could incorporate into a diabetes meal plan.

With the help of the ADA, we did it. And now, seven years later, we're doing it again. But this time, my team and I have revised the recipes so that they'll meet the ADA's updated nutritional guidelines.

I want to thank Rob Anthony, Director of Book Publishing, for his support of this project, and Managing Editor Abe Ogden for his insight and guidance in coordinating it all for the ADA. I appreciate the keen editorial work done by Laurie Guffey on our original edition, as well as that done by Rebecca Lanning, our editor for this edition. Thank you all for your caring attention to detail.

Once again, I owe so much to my editor and daughter Caryl Ginsburg Fantel, who oversees all my print projects; and to Howard Rosenthal for his ongoing creative input.

Of course, I must express my sincere appreciation to Joe Peppi, my Test Kitchen Supervisor, and to my top-notch recipe developers, Patty Rosenthal and Kirsten Schneider. You both have built upon the recipes in my original edition so masterfully.

Thanks, also, to the other members of my management and administrative staff. I couldn't do all this without you!

I want to express my appreciation once again to John Swanston for his assistance on behalf of Nicole. And, finally, a big thank-you to my family for their unwavering support, and to you, my fans, for urging me to create this book in the first place. I admire your courage and sincerely appreciate your loyalty. Together we can continue to do wonders!

Introduction

I'm no doctor or dietitian, but during the process of putting together this cookbook I learned a great deal about diabetes—both from professionals and from folks who deal with the difficulties of diabetes on a regular basis. I've compiled some basic information you'll need about food terms and package labels. I've also gathered some of the most commonly asked questions about diabetes, along with general answers for them. Then you'll find helpful hints on proper food portions; how to make great substitutions; the best ways to use sugar, artificial sweeteners, and sodium; and a note about packaged foods, but for more specifics on all of this, please consult your health care team.

Understanding Food Terms and Package Labels

Many food labels in the grocery store use terms that can be confusing. To help you shop and eat better, here is a list of the common terms as defined by the Food and Drug Administration.

Sugar

Sugar Free: Less than 0.5 grams of sugar per serving.
No Added Sugar, Without Added Sugar, No Sugar Added: This does not mean the same as "sugar free." A label bearing these words means that no sugars were added during processing, or that processing does not increase the sugar content above the amount the ingredients naturally contain. Consult the nutrition information panel to see the total amount of sugar in this product.
Reduced Sugar: At least 25% less sugar per serving than the regular product.

Calories

Calorie Free: Fewer than 5 calories per serving.
Low Calorie: 40 calories or less per serving. (If servings are smaller than 30 grams, or smaller than 2 tablespoons, this means 40 calories or less per 50 grams of food.)
Reduced Calorie, Fewer Calories: At least 25% fewer calories per serving than the regular product.

Fat

Fat Free, Nonfat: Less than 0.5 grams of fat per serving.
Low Fat: 3 grams or less of fat per serving. (If servings are smaller than 30 grams, or smaller than 2 tablespoons, this means 3 grams or less of fat per 50 grams of food.)
Reduced Fat, Less Fat: At least 25% less fat per serving than the regular product.

Cholesterol

Cholesterol Free: Less than 2 milligrams of cholesterol, and 2 grams or less of saturated fat per serving.
Low Cholesterol: 20 milligrams or less of cholesterol, and 2 grams or less of saturated fat per serving.
Reduced Cholesterol, Less Cholesterol: At least 25% less cholesterol, and 2 grams or less of saturated fat per serving than the regular product.

Sodium

Sodium Free: Less than 5 milligrams of sodium per serving.
Low Sodium: 140 milligrams or less of sodium per serving.
Very Low Sodium: 35 milligrams or less of sodium per serving.
Reduced Sodium, Less Sodium: At least 25% less sodium per serving than the regular product.

Light or Lite Foods

Foods that are labeled "Light" or "Lite" are usually either lower in fat or lower in calories than the regular product. Some products may also be lower in sodium. Check the nutrition information label on the back of the product to make sure.

Meat and Poultry

Lean: Less than 10 grams of fat, 4.5 grams or less of saturated fat, and less than 95 milligrams of cholesterol per serving and per 100 grams.
Extra Lean: Less than 5 grams of fat, less than 2 grams of saturated fat, and less than 95 milligrams of cholesterol per serving and per 100 grams.

One of the best ways we can help ourselves control diabetes through our diet is simply by reading the labels on food packages when we go shopping. Once we get past the name of a product and its claims of being lighter in one or more ingredients, there's more to examine. Food packaging may contain health claims that explain the value of the product. For example, a food high in fiber and low in saturated fat could be claimed to reduce cholesterol levels and, therefore, a person's risk of heart disease if he or she consumes that product. I can't stress enough that you should read food labels completely and carefully and, if you have any questions about particular foods, ask your physician or dietitian.

In addition to meeting requirements for the definitions of claims made on food labels, the FDA also requires that virtually all food labels contain a nutrition label, called Nutrition Facts.

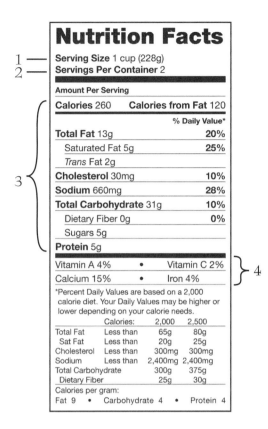

Nutrition Facts

Serving Size 1 cup (228g)
Servings Per Container 2

Amount Per Serving

Calories 260   Calories from Fat 120

% Daily Value*

Total Fat 13g   20%
   Saturated Fat 5g   25%
   Trans Fat 2g
Cholesterol 30mg   10%
Sodium 660mg   28%
Total Carbohydrate 31g   10%
   Dietary Fiber 0g   0%
   Sugars 5g
Protein 5g

Vitamin A 4%   •   Vitamin C 2%
Calcium 15%   •   Iron 4%

*Percent Daily Values are based on a 2,000
calorie diet. Your Daily Values may be higher or
lower depending on your calorie needs.

	Calories:	2,000	2,500
Total Fat	Less than	65g	80g
Sat Fat	Less than	20g	25g
Cholesterol	Less than	300mg	300mg
Sodium	Less than	2,400mg	2,400mg
Total Carbohydrate		300g	375g
Dietary Fiber		25g	30g

Calories per gram:
Fat 9   •   Carbohydrate 4   •   Protein 4

Source: U.S. Food and Drug Administration

1 Serving Size—This is what is considered to be standard for the item. You may find that your serving size fluctuates quite a bit depending upon how small or large a serving you and your family eat of a particular item. Please be realistic here and remember that portion control is a big factor in diabetes management.

2 Servings Per Container—Again, the servings are just a guideline of what is considered average. This number should be adjusted depending on your personal dietary needs.

3 To most of us, the important information is the amount of fat, cholesterol, sodium, carbohydrates, and nutrients contained in any food. That's why these are listed not only in grams or milligrams, but also as a percentage of an average person's daily allotment, based on a daily 2,000-calorie (or sometimes also a 2,500-calorie) diet. Your own daily values for these items may be higher or lower, depending on your level of activity and your personal needs. Please note that since carbohydrates are found in sugar and starch, this is the main cause of increased blood glucose levels. The ADA recommends that people with diabetes follow the federal government's guidelines for healthy adults and consume no more than 45 to 65% of total daily calories as carbohydrates.

4 Only two vitamins, A and C, and two minerals, calcium and iron, are required to be listed on food labels. Food companies may voluntarily list others and, if they do, make that information work for you!

You shouldn't have to look too hard for nutrition information, because the government regulates the size of the labels. It also has strict guidelines regarding the information that is contained in these labels. This means that we can count on their being large and clear enough to read and understand easily. Okay, we're set with the reading part—but what about the understanding part?

The sample nutritional fact label on the previous page offers a clear explanation of what those numbers mean to us.

Some labels also list the approximate number of calories in a gram of fat, carbohydrate, and protein. When available, these numbers can be helpful in creating your meal plans.

Since the format of and information contained on food labels is supposed to be consistent from product to product and brand to brand, you can do your own comparisons and balance your food choices. Few foods provide 100% of a single nutrient, so the percentage values on the packages can help us make knowledgeable nutrition choices. As always, if you'd like further information on how to shape your own meal plan, the best place to start is with your physician and/or registered dietitian.

Frequently Asked Questions

1. **I keep seeing the abbreviation RD in my information pamphlets. What is an RD, and why do I need to see one?**
    RD is the abbreviation for Registered Dietitian. Now don't think of an RD as the "food police," but rather a personal nutritional guidance counselor. In a nutshell, RDs are trained to analyze how your body uses food, and armed with that information, they offer practical ways on how to manage your particular meal plan and control your blood sugars. Your RD will be able to help you come up with tantalizing meal plans, share tips on how to make bland foods "pop," determine what your daily calorie goal is, and answer your food-related questions. Staying in touch with your dietitian will keep you up-to-date on the latest nutritional recommendations. Your physician or local hospital can get you hooked up with an RD in your area.

2. **Can I still go out with my friends once in a while for a beer?**
    Most people with diabetes do not have to swear off alcohol, but remember: MODERATION IS KEY. One drink is defined as a 5-ounce glass of wine, a 12-ounce light beer, or 1-1/2 ounces of 80-proof distilled spirits. The ADA generally recommends no more than two drinks a day for men and one drink a day for women. Always make sure you know what is in your drink. Example: piña coladas and other rum drinks and drinks with fruit juice are very high in sugar, and may affect your blood sugar levels more than beer or wine. Make sure you eat something while you're having a drink, because consuming alcohol on an empty stomach makes it more likely that you'll develop hypoglycemia.

3. **What vitamins should I be taking to help my diabetes?**

   More studies need to be done on this, but many doctors believe a person with diabetes who eats a good variety of fruits, veggies, and meats each day really shouldn't need to supplement his or her diet with vitamins. If you decide to take supplements, check with your physician or RD before adding them to your meal plan.

4. **Can weight loss really help me?**

   How could it NOT help most of us?! Not only does being close to your target weight improve blood pressure and blood fat levels, reducing the risk of heart disease, but it also lowers the chances of your body impeding the effects of insulin. Often a bonus of weight control is the ability to cut back on medications. Why not make attaining your ideal weight your personal goal?

5. **Nicole, with your demanding schedule as Miss America, how did you manage to stay on track with your meal plan?**

   Demanding is an understatement, but during my reign as Miss America, I had to make a commitment to test my blood glucose level often to stay in control of my diabetes. Honestly, it's still a struggle for me, and many times I don't feel like doing it, but I know it is necessary for my life and my busy lifestyle. I have testing equipment in all my travel bags and in my car, which helps avoid logistical problems, and I wear an insulin pump, which helps tremendously. Concerning my meal plan, I have learned that I don't have to be restricted to printed menus—you can always request different combinations of foods prepared the way you want them in restaurants. I also exercise anywhere I can, even in shopping malls or hotel stairwells!

6. **What foods can I splurge on?**

   Well, sitting in front of the TV with a box of chocolates is out of the question—like it is for all people who want to be healthy! Yes, I know it is so hard to stay on track while it seems like people all around you are eating anything and everything they want. You can indulge a little, but what's my key word? MODERATION. That means practicing portion control (get help from the portion size table on page 8) and keeping track of what you eat during the day. If you eat well (translation: within your individual guidelines) during the day, then you just may be able to reward yourself a bit at dinner . . . and I mean just a bit. It's easy to be creative with your meal planning. As you go through the recipes in this book, you'll see that healthy eating doesn't have to be boring. And, before you know it, you'll be glad you made the commitment to healthy eating—and living!

7. **Are all fats the same? Please end my confusion!**

   No, all fats are *NOT* the same, nor are they all bad! In fact, small amounts of some fats are actually beneficial to us. For instance, the fat found in nuts like almonds, pistachios, peanuts, and cashews, and also avocados and olive and canola oils, is called monounsaturated. It is believed that this fat raises our HDL (good) cholesterol and lowers our LDL (bad) cholesterol levels. The next healthiest for us are the polyunsaturated fats. These are found mainly in vegetable oil, and they are also thought to lower LDL levels. You'll want to limit saturated (solid) fats, like those found in meat fat, lard, and, sorry, bacon, and avoid trans fats, which are found in processed foods. These types of fat cause blood cholesterol to rise. In general, a healthy meal plan includes 25 to 35% of calories from fat, with less than 7% of those derived from saturated fat and as little trans fat as possible.

8. **Nicole, what advice would you give kids to help them deal with friends, family, and others who don't understand diabetes?**

Unless someone lives with this condition, they cannot fully understand its psychological, emotional, and physical effects. There will always be people who just can't grasp what diabetes is, so don't sweat it. One of the keys to overcoming your sense of isolation is to get plugged into a group with kids your age who have diabetes or face a similar challenge. A good support system is key to diabetes care and control.

9. **What should I do in case I am stuck somewhere without my insulin?**

Excellent question! Where I live in south Florida, storms can cut off power for days. It's been drilled into our heads to have emergency supplies always on hand and available. You should, too, no matter where you live. Insulin lasts for at least a month at room temperature, but if exposed to bright light, freezing or extremely hot conditions, it could lose its effectiveness. In the event that you are physically working harder and not eating as much, monitor your glucose carefully, and adjust your insulin dosage. There is a book called *Planning Your Diabetes Care During Disaster Conditions*, prepared by the Garden State Association of Diabetes Educators. It offers tips and advice in case you find yourself in a dilemma. It is available online at *www.bddiabetes.com*, or you can order it from Becton Dickinson Consumer Services at 1-800-237-4554.

10. **Are sweet foods gone forever for me?**

Not at all! You don't have to say "no" to that small slice of chocolate birthday cake; just adjust for it by eating a little less bread that day and perhaps taking a quick walk around the block. Basically, if you eat too much sugar—or ANY carbohydrate-containing food, even pasta or potatoes—your blood glucose level will jump higher. Sugar contains "empty" calories, those without vitamins, minerals, or fiber, which don't help you at all, and cause you to gain weight. Instead of using large amounts of sugar in your foods, experiment with different types of fruit juices, spices and seasonings, or even applesauce. Small amounts of sugar are generally okay, but if you're trying to eat fewer calories, artificial sweeteners might also help you to satisfy your sweet tooth. Take a look at pages 10 through 12.

11. **If I ate the same things every day, wouldn't my glucose control be easier?**
Yes, but can you say "boring"? Everybody needs variety, and, really, tasty meals can be nutritious, too. Experiment with different foods by taking your blood glucose levels about an hour after you eat, and find out how different foods affect you. Your RD can prepare meal plans that will help keep you healthy and out of that same-old-meal rut.

12. **How can I cut the fat in my diet?**
Here are some tips that can be easily worked into your program. First, try to avoid fried foods. Go for lean meat and veggies that have been baked, broiled, or roasted. Stir-fry with lots of seasonings and a tiny amount of oil. Use canola oil or olive oil instead of lard. And here's the easiest of all: Choose low-fat or fat-free foods instead of regular foods. That's not so hard, huh?

13. **I have a big family event coming up. What do I do if I overeat?**
Hit the road, Jack! Literally. Assuming that your doctor has given you the okay to exercise, lace up your sneakers and go for a walk. I don't mean a leisurely stroll, either. Make it brisk, if your doctor approves! And, while you're at it, take someone with you. Exercising is much more pleasant with a buddy, and, chances are, you're not the only one who's splurged and needs a spin around the block. Even if you haven't binged (and we all do at one time or another), one or two walks a day will contribute to lowering your blood glucose levels.

14. **What is the difference between hypo- and hyperglycemia?**
It's very important to know the difference between these two, because the treatment is different. Hypoglycemia is when blood sugars fall too low. This can be caused by alcohol, too much insulin, or not eating enough. Symptoms can include sweating, turning pale, having trouble paying attention, and a tingling sensation around the mouth. If this happens, quickly drink something with sugar in it, like regular soda or juice, or eat a piece of candy. Hyperglycemia is having too much glucose (sugar) in the blood. Not enough insulin, overeating, and stress can all contribute to an attack. Signs include tiredness, excessive thirst, frequent urination, upset stomach, and a fruity smell to the breath. Treat with extra insulin, or less food. More serious cases require immediate medical attention.

Portion Pointers

What do a tennis ball, a light bulb, and a computer mouse have in common? Keep reading and you'll find out.

Is it really such a big deal if you eat a smidgen more than what your meal plan calls for? You might think that an extra ounce of something here or there won't really affect anything, but put down that fork, because it *does* make a difference. Those extra calories add up, bringing you extra weight, making it that much harder to control diabetes. That's where portion control comes in.

I certainly don't expect anyone to run around with a food scale, so here are two easy ways you can measure your foods:

■ Try this with fruits and veggies: In the supermarket produce section, pick up small, medium, and large pieces of fruit in your hands and guesstimate their weight; then weigh them on the store's scale. How close are you? After doing this a few times, you'll be able to fairly accurately guess the weight of most fruit and veggies. That's the start of portion control!

■ Say you want to know what 1 cup of low-fat milk looks like. Will you always have to use a measuring cup? No way! Simply measure one cup of any liquid in a measuring cup, then pour the liquid into one of your regular drinking glasses. Mark or memorize where the liquid comes up to. It's so easy! This method can actually be applied to just about anything, from how much cereal to put in your bowl to how much oil you use to coat your skillet. It's always best to be aware of exactly what you're taking in.

When you eat out, portion control can get a bit tricky. If you go to a restaurant that serves large portions, then split your meal with your partner, or, better yet, right when your meal arrives, set aside half to bring home for lunch or dinner the next day. Now for the tennis ball, light bulb, and computer mouse part. Here's a table that references everyday objects to help you compare food portions:

2 tablespoons salad dressing	=	ice cube
3 ounces meat	=	deck of cards
medium apple	=	tennis ball
medium potato	=	computer mouse
medium onion	=	baseball
1 cup cut fruit	=	average orange
1 ounce meat	=	matchbox
1/2 cup cooked pasta	=	ice cream scoop
1 ounce bread	=	CD case
1 cup broccoli	=	light bulb
2 tablespoons peanut butter	=	golf ball
1 ounce cheese	=	domino

After practicing these tips, you'll be able to tell the sizes of your portions just by looking at them. It's really not that hard, and, speaking of cards, balls, and dominoes, you can even turn it into a game! The winner? You, of course!

Substitution Savvy

Okay, so you have to make a few adjustments in your eating habits. Does that mean you'll have to give up tasty foods? No way! Making the switch from the traditional versions of your favorite foods to their lower-fat counterparts can be a snap, and I bet you're already using some lower-calorie foods. Keep going with that, and use this sensible guide to help you use healthier foods without losing the flavor you long for.

Instead of	Try this
Full-fat cheese	Low- or reduced-fat cheese, or a strong-flavored cheese (with those you can usually use half the amount a recipe calls for)
Regular fried corn or potato chips	Baked tortilla or potato chips, or pretzels
Heavy cream	Evaporated skim milk
Croissants	Bagels, pita bread
Whole eggs	Egg substitute, egg whites
Ground beef	Lean ground beef, ground turkey breast
Ice cream	Sherbet, frozen yogurt, low-fat ice cream
Sour cream	Fat-free sour cream or plain yogurt
Whole milk	Fat-free or 1% milk

Substituting lower-calorie foods is only one step in healthier eating, but there are several ways we can prepare or cook our meals that will make them better for us. Here are a few ideas.

■ Instead of frying or sautéing, give baking, steaming, poaching, broiling, or grilling a try. These methods really cut down on fat.

■ Use nonstick pots and pans because they require less fat to keep food from sticking.

■ Add a splash of citrus juice—lemon, lime, or orange—to dressings to give them zing without adding calories.

■ With strong-flavored cheeses like blue, Parmesan, and Romano, simply cut down on the amount used; a little of those goes a long way!

- If you are limiting dietary cholesterol, eggs can still be a part of your meal plan, but in moderation. Two egg whites equal one whole egg, and there are also great egg substitutes in the egg section of your grocery store. Give those a try.

- When eating at home or eating out, watch what you drink! Drink water, unsweetened brewed iced tea, or unsweetened sparkling water instead of soft drinks, sugar-laden fruit juices, or milk shakes. A slice of fresh lemon or lime will add a zip to your water or iced tea, too.

- In restaurants, choose steamed vegetables instead of fat-laden side dishes, and ask for dressings, sauces, and condiments (low-fat and low-calorie, when possible) on the side so you can control your intake.

I know you're not going to make all these changes overnight, but given some time and a little practice, you'll have no problems putting together great-tasting, good-for-you meals. Trust me!

Sugar and Artificial Sweeteners

One of the first thoughts that goes through a person's head after being diagnosed with diabetes is, "Oh, no! I can never have anything sweet again!" Well, that was how it was years ago, when doctors believed that regular table sugar (sucrose) made blood glucose levels fly through the roof.

Hence, the arrival of artificial sweeteners. Along with their commercial availability came a slew of questions and concerns, such as "Can I bake with them?" and "Are they better for me than sugar?" I like to call these sweeteners "freebies" because they sweeten our foods without adding calories and raising blood glucose levels.

Before I tell you more about artificial sweeteners, you should know that, thanks to extensive testing, the American Diabetes Association changed its nutritional recommendations in 1994 and reported that sugar doesn't affect blood glucose much differently than any other carbohydrate.

Now don't go running out for a jumbo candy bar just yet. The ADA report stated that sugar could indeed be worked into diabetic meal plans set up by dietitians, with the understanding that sugar is not a "free food." Sugar counts as a carbohydrate and must therefore be substituted for other foods containing carbohydrates. And since sugar calories are "empty" calories, it's certainly preferable to choose carbohydrates that provide more nutritive value. *That's* why we can have sugar—in moderation.

Since many people with diabetes still use quite a lot of artificial sweeteners, let's take a look at four that are currently ADA- and Food and Drug Administration–approved:

1. Although there has been debate over its use since the early 1900s, **saccharin** is the most commonly used artificial sweetener in the United States. With a taste

300 times sweeter than sugar, saccharin, found in Sweet 'N Low®, works well in both hot and cold dishes.

2. **Aspartame**, a.k.a. NutraSweet® and Equal®, was discovered in 1965. Mild reactions, such as headaches and dizziness, have been reported from the use of aspartame, and people with PKU (phenylketonuria, a rare genetic disease) must avoid anything containing it. Aspartame tends to lose its sweetness when heated for long periods, so, when possible, it should be added to baked items toward the end of cooking, or sprinkled on after their removal from the heat.

3. Acesulfame-K, also known as **acesulfame potassium**, is sold under the brand name Sweet One®. Discovered in 1967, this sweetener is 200 times sweeter than sugar. Sweet One contains 1 gram of carbohydrate. Acesulfame-K can be used in baking, but produces finished items with a noticeably different texture than those made with sugar.

4. **Sucralose** is 600 times sweeter than sugar. This sweetener, known by the brand name Splenda®, is made from sugar and contains carbohydrates. People have been very successful cooking and baking with it, and it can also be added directly to foods.

Here's a helpful chart that converts sugar measurements to numbers of packets of no-calorie sweeteners. Many of the recipes in this book work well with either sugar or artificial sweetener. However, please note that since sugar is important to the volume and texture of most baked goods, you may find that you can replace only half the amount of sugar called for in a baked goods recipe with an appropriate sugar substitute. Experiment and see for yourself. **Don't forget: Moderate use of sugar is approved by the ADA in the majority of diabetic meal plans; use what works for your particular plan.**

Sugar amount		*Equivalency in sweetener packets*
2 teaspoons	=	1 packet
1 tablespoon	=	1-1/2 packets
1/4 cup	=	6 packets
1/3 cup	=	8 packets
1/2 cup	=	12 packets
3/4 cup	=	18 packets
1 cup	=	24 packets
1 pound	=	57 packets

Remember that everyone reacts differently to various sweeteners, so discuss their use with your physician and dietitian, and use what works for you. And whether you choose to use sugar or artificial sweeteners—or a combination—test your blood glucose levels after you eat all sweet foods in order to determine their effect on you. Also ask your physician about increasing your insulin intake at those times when you know you will be eating sweet foods. Our goal with eating sweet foods should be to make sure they're physician- or dietitian-approved and as nutritious as possible.

Sodium Smarts

Did you know that our bodies require only about 220 mg of sodium (salt) per day, yet the average American takes in almost 5,000 mg per day? Wow! We really like our salt, huh? The American Diabetes Association recommends that people with diabetes (and actually everyone) keep their daily sodium intake to less than 2,300 mg, and those with mild or moderate hypertension stay under 1,500 mg per day.

We shouldn't cut sodium out of our diets completely, as our bodies need it to function properly. And what's my favorite word? MODERATION! Too little of most things is no good, and too much isn't good, either. Too much sodium can raise blood pressure, which in turn can raise the chances of developing heart disease or stroke.

So, you want to know how you're supposed to season your food without adding measurable amounts of sodium, right? That's easy! With a clove or two of chopped or pressed garlic, some onion, and, of course, fresh herbs. It can be so much fun to experiment with them, especially since fresh herbs are almost always available in the supermarket produce section.

Here's a simple seasoning trick that I've been using lately: using canned reduced-fat, low-sodium chicken broth in place of water when making rice or pasta—or just about anything that needs a little liquid. Keep a few cans on hand to help flavor almost anything you cook!

A Note about Packaged Foods

Packaged food sizes may vary by brand. Generally, the sizes indicated in these recipes are average sizes. If you can't find the exact package size listed in the ingredients, whatever package is closest in size will usually work in the recipe, but please remember that using different products may alter the recipe's nutritional analysis. Experiment with different brands until you're satisfied.

As I mention throughout this book, always use the lightest ingredients possible. And just because a product's name includes the word "light" doesn't necessarily make it so. You need to read and know what you're looking for on package labels. (See "Understanding Food Terms and Package Labels" on page 1.) It's the best way to truly start lightening up your diet.

Bunch o' Munchies

Parmesan–Spinach Dip

2 packages (10 ounces each) frozen chopped spinach, thawed and squeezed dry

1 package (8 ounces) reduced-fat cream cheese, softened

1 package (8 ounces) fat-free cream cheese, softened

1/2 cup freshly grated Parmesan cheese (1 tablespoon reserved for topping)

1/3 cup fat-free mayonnaise

2 tablespoons fresh lemon juice

1 teaspoon garlic powder

1 can (8 ounces) sliced water chestnuts, drained and chopped

1 Preheat the oven to 350°F. Coat a 9-inch pie plate with nonstick cooking spray.

2 In a medium bowl, beat the spinach, cream cheese, all but the reserved 1 tablespoon Parmesan cheese, the mayonnaise, lemon juice, and garlic powder until well blended. Stir in the water chestnuts, then spoon the mixture into the pie plate.

3 Sprinkle the dip with the reserved 1 tablespoon Parmesan cheese, then cover with aluminum foil and bake for 15 minutes; remove the foil and cook for 15 to 20 more minutes, or until heated through. Serve immediately.

Exchanges

1 Vegetable
1/2 Fat

Calories	42
Calories from Fat	19
Total Fat	2 g
Saturated Fat	1.4 g
Cholesterol	8 mg
Sodium	146 mg
Total Carbohydrate	3 g
Dietary Fiber	1 g
Sugars	1 g
Protein	3 g

"What a combo—this dip and almost anything! It goes really well with Garlic Pita Crisps (page 29), toasted thin bagel slices, and fresh-cut vegetables."

Roasted Red Pepper Dip

Serving Size: 2 tablespoons, Total Servings: 12

- **1** jar (7 ounces) roasted red peppers, drained and patted dry
- **1** container (8 ounces) reduced-fat sour cream
- **1** container (8 ounces) fat-free sour cream
- **1** tablespoon chopped fresh basil
- **1** garlic clove
- **1/8** teaspoon black pepper

1. Place all the ingredients in a blender jar and process until thoroughly blended. Serve immediately, or store in the refrigerator in an airtight container until ready to use.

Note

Serve with assorted fresh-cut vegetables for dipping. If you want to roast your own peppers, cut 3 medium bell peppers (any color) into 1-inch strips. In a medium bowl, combine 2 tablespoons olive oil and 1/4 teaspoon each of garlic powder, onion powder, salt, and black pepper. Add the pepper strips and toss to coat, then place in a 9" × 13" baking dish and bake in a preheated 450°F. oven for 20 to 25 minutes, or until the peppers are fork-tender.

Exchanges
1 Vegetable
1/2 Fat

Calories	45
Calories from Fat	15
Total Fat	2 g
Saturated Fat	1.3 g
Cholesterol	9 mg
Sodium	63 mg
Total Carbohydrate	3 g
Dietary Fiber	0 g
Sugars	2 g
Protein	3 g

"Keep track of the portions you eat, whether you're snacking, or at a tailgate, cocktail, or dinner party. Even though this dip is awesome tasting, too much dipping could upset your meal plan. Remember, moderation is key with any type of healthy eating, but especially for people with diabetes, like us."

"Dill-lightful" Lemon Dip

Serving Size: 2 tablespoons, Total Servings: 12

1 cup light mayonnaise

1/2 cup buttermilk

1 teaspoon fresh lemon juice

1 tablespoon chopped fresh dill

1/2 teaspoon garlic powder

1/4 teaspoon black pepper

1/2 teaspoon grated lemon peel

1 In a small bowl, whisk together all the ingredients until well combined. Serve, or cover and chill until ready to serve.

Serving Tips

Cook up some cleaned fresh asparagus spears a few minutes in the microwave, then chill them until ready to dip. You might also want to dollop this sparingly on your grilled fish or chicken.

Exchanges
1-1/2 Fat

Calories 71
Calories from Fat . . . 61
Total Fat . . . . 7 g
Saturated Fat . . . . 1 g
Cholesterol . . . . 7 mg
Sodium . . . . 171 mg
Total Carbohydrate . . . 2 g
Dietary Fiber . . . . 0 g
Sugars . . . . 1 g
Protein . . . . 0 g

Garlic-Lover's Hummus

Serving Size: 1/4 cup, Total Servings: 10

2 cans (15 ounces each) garbanzo beans (chickpeas), rinsed, with 1/3 cup original liquid reserved

3 garlic cloves

2 tablespoons fresh lemon juice

2 tablespoons olive oil

1 teaspoon ground cumin

1 teaspoon salt

1 Combine all the ingredients, including the reserved garbanzo bean liquid, in a food processor that has been fitted with its metal cutting blade. Process until the mixture is smooth and creamy and no lumps remain, scraping down the sides of the bowl as needed.

2 Serve immediately, or cover and chill until ready to use.

Did You Know ...

that the garbanzo bean is as important to the peoples of India, North Africa, and the Middle East as the potato is to Americans? It's a traditional food eaten in many different ways. This Middle Eastern favorite is most often served with pita bread triangles or cracker bread, but fresh-cut veggies like broccoli and cauliflower florets and carrot sticks team well with it, too.

Exchanges
1 Starch
1 Fat

Calories 122
Calories from Fat . . . 33
Total Fat . . . . 4 g
Saturated Fat . . . . 1 g
Cholesterol . . . . 0 mg
Sodium . . . . 403 mg
Total Carbohydrate . . 18 g
Dietary Fiber . . . . 4 g
Sugars . . . . 2 g
Protein . . . . 5 g

Quick-Step Salsa

Serving Size: 1/4 cup, Total Servings: 10

2 large ripe tomatoes, finely chopped

1/2 medium-sized green bell pepper, finely chopped

1 small onion, finely chopped

1 teaspoon hot pepper sauce

1/4 teaspoon ground cumin

2 tablespoons chopped fresh cilantro

1 In a medium bowl, combine all the ingredients; mix well.

2 Cover and chill for at least 1 hour, or until ready to serve. (This should last up to 1 week if kept refrigerated in an airtight container.)

Exchanges
Free Food

Calories 13
Calories from Fat 1
Total Fat . . . . 0 g
Saturated Fat . . . . 0 g
Cholesterol . . . . 0 mg
Sodium . . . . 7 mg
Total Carbohydrate . . . 3 g
Dietary Fiber . . . . 1 g
Sugars . . . . 2 g
Protein . . . . 0 g

"This south-of-the-border favorite is light and zesty enough to put a swing in your step. And paired with fresh veggies or baked tortilla chips, it's sure to have the gang saying 'iAy caramba!' (which means 'WOW!' in Spanish)."

Marinated Steak Nachos

1/2 cup lemon juice

2 tablespoons minced garlic

1 tablespoon dried oregano

1 tablespoon ground cumin

1 teaspoon salt

1 tablespoon black pepper

1 1-pound beef flank steak, trimmed of excess fat

1 package (14 ounces) baked fat-free tortilla chips

1/2 cup (2 ounces) shredded reduced-fat Colby Jack cheese blend

2 medium tomatoes, seeded and chopped

3 scallions, thinly sliced

1 In a 9" × 13" baking dish, combine the lemon juice, garlic, oregano, cumin, salt, and pepper. Add the steak, turning to coat completely. Cover and marinate in the refrigerator for 30 minutes.

2 Preheat the broiler. Place the steak on a rimmed baking sheet, discarding the marinade. Broil for 8 to 9 minutes per side for medium, or until desired doneness beyond that. Allow to cool for 10 minutes. Place on a cutting board and cut across the grain into thin slices, then cut into 1-inch pieces. Reduce the oven temperature to 350°F.

3 Spread the tortilla chips over two large rimmed baking sheets, then top evenly with the sliced steak and sprinkle with the cheese. Bake for 5 to 6 minutes, or until the cheese is melted. Remove from the oven and slide onto a large platter, if desired; sprinkle with the tomatoes and scallions. Serve immediately.

Exchanges
2 Starch
1 Lean Meat

Calories 197
  Calories from Fat . . . 37
Total Fat . . . . 74 g
  Saturated Fat . . . . . . 1.4 g
Cholesterol . . . . 16 mg
Sodium . . . . 293 mg
Total Carbohydrate . . 30 g
  Dietary Fiber . . . . 5 g
  Sugars . . . . 1 g
Protein . . . . 12 g

"The photo on the opposite page gives you a preview of how tempting these look when they come out of the oven. (Sometimes I even top them with jalapeño peppers.) Don't you want to dig right in?!"

Marinated Steak Nachos

A

Turkey Française

B

Steak Provençal

C

Lasagna Primavera

D

Mexican Tortilla Soup

Asian Wraps

Serving Size: 2 wraps, Total Servings: 10

3/4 pound boneless, skinless chicken breast, cooked and shredded

1/4 pound fresh bean sprouts

1/2 small head Napa or Chinese cabbage, shredded (about 3 cups)

1 medium carrot, shredded (about 1 cup)

6 scallions, thinly sliced

1/4 cup white vinegar

3 tablespoons canola oil

2 tablespoons light soy sauce

1 tablespoon sesame oil

2 garlic cloves, minced

2 teaspoons ground ginger

1/2 teaspoon black pepper

1 to 2 heads Bibb lettuce, separated to obtain 20 leaves

1 In a large bowl, combine the chicken, bean sprouts, cabbage, carrot, and scallions; mix well.

2 In a small bowl, combine the vinegar, canola oil, soy sauce, sesame oil, garlic, ginger, and black pepper; mix well and pour over the cabbage mixture. Mix until evenly coated.

3 Spoon an equal amount of the chicken mixture onto the center of each lettuce leaf and fold like an envelope. Turn over and place on a serving platter.

Exchanges
1 Vegetable
1 Lean Meat
1 Fat

Calories 123
  Calories from Fat . . . 61
Total Fat . . . . 7 g
  Saturated Fat . . . . . . 0.8 g
Cholesterol . . . . 29 mg
Sodium . . . . 156 mg
Total Carbohydrate . . . 4 g
  Dietary Fiber . . . . 1 g
  Sugars . . . . 2 g
Protein . . . . 12 g

"For your next party, why not serve up some fun by putting out the chicken mixture and the lettuce leaves and letting everybody fold their own wraps?! Not only is this a time-saver for you, but it lets the gang in on the action, too."

Eggplant Pizza Chips

Serving Size: 3 chips, Total Servings: 8

2 eggs

1 tablespoon water

1/4 teaspoon black pepper

1-1/4 cups Italian-flavored bread crumbs

1 large eggplant, peeled and cut into 1/4-inch rounds

Nonstick cooking spray

2 cups light spaghetti sauce (see box)

1/2 cup (2 ounces) shredded reduced-fat mozzarella cheese (see box)

1 Preheat the oven to 350°F. In a shallow dish, beat the eggs with the water and the pepper. Place the bread crumbs in another shallow dish. Line 2 large baking sheets with aluminum foil and coat generously with nonstick cooking spray; set aside.

2 Dip each eggplant round in the egg mixture, then in the bread crumbs, coating completely. Place on the baking sheets in a single layer, then spray the tops with nonstick cooking spray. Bake for 15 minutes, then turn the slices over and spray the other side with the nonstick cooking spray; bake for 15 more minutes.

3 Remove from the oven and place about 1 tablespoon spaghetti sauce on each. Sprinkle evenly with mozzarella cheese and return to the oven for 4 to 5 more minutes, or until the sauce is bubbly and the cheese is melted.

Exchanges
1 Starch
2 Vegetable
1/2 Fat

Calories 148
  Calories from Fat . . . 34
Total Fat . . . . 4 g
  Saturated Fat . . . . . . 1.4 g
Cholesterol . . . . 57 mg
Sodium . . . . 642 mg
Total Carbohydrate . . 22 g
  Dietary Fiber . . . . 3 g
  Sugars . . . . 6 g
Protein . . . . 7 g

"You can substitute other kinds of cheese, if you'd prefer, and if you want to serve these 'naked,' just leave off the spaghetti sauce."

Spicy Glazed Meatballs

Serving Size: 3 meatballs, Total Servings: 8

1 pound extra-lean ground turkey breast

1 small onion, finely chopped

1/2 medium-sized green bell pepper, finely chopped

1/4 cup shredded wheat cereal, finely crushed

2 egg whites

1/2 teaspoon garlic powder

1/4 teaspoon ground red pepper

1/2 teaspoon salt

1/4 teaspoon black pepper

1 tablespoon canola oil

1/4 cup jalapeño pepper jelly, melted

1 In a medium bowl, combine the turkey, onion, bell pepper, cereal, egg whites, garlic powder, ground red pepper, salt, and black pepper. Shape into 24 one-inch meatballs.

2 Heat the oil in a large skillet over medium heat. Add the meatballs, cover, and cook for 8 to 10 minutes, or until no pink remains, turning occasionally to brown on all sides.

3 In a large bowl, combine the meatballs and the melted jalapeño pepper jelly, tossing to coat completely. Serve immediately by placing on individual plates if an appetizer, or on a platter with toothpicks if an hors d'oeuvre.

Did You Know . . .

that there's a difference between ground turkey breast and just plain ground turkey? Ground turkey breast usually has less fat and cholesterol, so read package labels carefully before making your choices.

Exchanges
1/2 Carbohydrate
2 Very Lean Meat

Calories 115
    Calories from Fat . . . 20
Total Fat . . . . 2 g
    Saturated Fat . . . . 0 g
Cholesterol . . . . 35 mg
Sodium . . . . 200 mg
Total Carbohydrate . . . 8 g
    Dietary Fiber . . . . 0 g
    Sugars . . . . 6 g
Protein . . . . 15 g

Kickin' Onion Chicken Tenders

Serving Size: 3 strips, Total Servings: 8

1 cup cornflake crumbs

1 tablespoon dried flaked minced onion

1/2 cup hot cayenne pepper sauce

1-1/2 pounds boneless, skinless chicken breasts, cut into 24 strips

Nonstick cooking spray

1 Preheat the oven to 450°F. Coat two baking sheets with nonstick cooking spray.

2 Mix the cornflake crumbs and minced onion together and place in a shallow dish. Place the hot sauce in its own shallow dish. Dip the chicken strips into the hot sauce, then into the cornflake mix, coating evenly with each.

3 Place the coated strips on the baking sheets and spray the tops with cooking spray. Bake for 10 to 12 minutes, or until no pink remains in the chicken. Serve immediately.

Exchanges
1/2 Starch
3 Lean Meat

Calories 142
　Calories from Fat . . . 19
Total Fat . . . . 2 g
　Saturated Fat . . . . . . 0.6 g
Cholesterol . . . . 49 mg
Sodium . . . . 250 mg
Total Carbohydrate . . 10 g
　Dietary Fiber . . . . 0 g
　Sugars . . . . 1 g
Protein . . . . 19 g

"No bones about it, these are the perfect flavor-packed munchie for when you and the gang kick up your feet and get into the big game. (Give your hands a good wipe before grabbing that remote!)"

Chicken "Ribs"

1 can (10-1/2 ounces) condensed beef broth

1/4 cup ketchup

1/4 cup honey

1/4 cup light soy sauce

4 garlic cloves, minced

1/8 teaspoon red food color

2 pounds boneless, skinless chicken thighs, cut into strips

1 In a large bowl, combine all the ingredients. Cover and chill overnight, or for at least 4 hours.

2 Preheat the oven to 450°F. Line a rimmed baking sheet with aluminum foil. Place the chicken strips on the baking sheet, discarding the remaining marinade.

3 Bake for 10 minutes, then turn the chicken over; bake for 8 to 10 more minutes, or until no pink remains in the chicken and it is glazed. Serve immediately.

Exchanges
3 Very Lean Meat

Calories 106
　Calories from Fat . . . 18
Total Fat . . . . 2 g
　Saturated Fat . . . . 1 g
Cholesterol . . . . 46 mg
Sodium . . . . 214 mg
Total Carbohydrate . . . 4 g
　Dietary Fiber . . . . 0 g
　Sugars . . . . 4 g
Protein . . . . 17 g

On-the-Money Clams Casino

1/4 pound raw bacon

1/2 small red bell pepper, coarsely chopped

2 garlic cloves

1/4 cup Italian-flavored bread crumbs

1 tablespoon grated Parmesan cheese

2 dozen littleneck clams

1 In a food processor that has been fitted with its metal cutting blade, combine the bacon, red pepper, and garlic; process until smooth. Add the bread crumbs and cheese and continue to process until thoroughly mixed and the mixture holds together; set aside.

2 Meanwhile, in a large pot, bring 2 inches of water to a boil. Place the clams in the boiling water. Cover the pot and steam the clams for 5 to 8 minutes, or until they open. Place the clams on a platter. **Discard any clams that do not open.**

3 Preheat the broiler. Remove the top shells of the clams and discard, leaving the clams in the bottom halves of the shells. Evenly divide and spread the bread crumb mixture over the clams, completely covering them. Place on a baking sheet and broil for 4 to 6 minutes, or until the topping is cooked through.

Exchanges
1/2 Starch
2 Very Lean Meat
1/2 Fat

Calories 112
  Calories from Fat . . . 32
Total Fat . . . . 4 g
  Saturated Fat . . . . . . 1.1 g
Cholesterol . . . . 33 mg
Sodium . . . . 258 mg
Total Carbohydrate . . . 6 g
  Dietary Fiber . . . . 0 g
  Sugars . . . . 2 g
Protein . . . . 13 g

Good for You!

*Fishing for compliments?
Not only will your guests be clamoring for more of this appetizer, but clams (and mussels, too) are swimming with nutrients and have practically no saturated fat!*

Sweet 'n' Spicy Shrimp

Serving Size: 4 to 5 shrimp, Total Servings: 6

2 tablespoons honey

1 tablespoon yellow mustard

1/2 teaspoon dried minced onion

1/4 teaspoon ground ginger

1 tablespoon butter

1 pound large shrimp (24 to 30 count), peeled and deveined

2 teaspoons fresh chopped parsley

1 In a small bowl, combine the honey, mustard, minced onion, and ginger; mix well and set aside.

2 In a large skillet, melt the butter over medium heat and sauté the shrimp for 1 to 2 minutes. Add the honey-mustard mixture to the shrimp, stirring until the shrimp are pink and the sauce is heated through.

3 Sprinkle with the chopped parsley and serve immediately.

Exchanges
1/2 Carbohydrate
2 Very Lean Meat

Calories 95
  Calories from Fat . . . 23
Total Fat . . . . 3 g
  Saturated Fat . . . . 1 g
Cholesterol . . . . 112 mg
Sodium . . . . 174 mg
Total Carbohydrate . . . 6 g
  Dietary Fiber . . . . 0 g
  Sugars . . . . 6 g
Protein . . . . 12 g

"When shopping for shrimp for this recipe, be sure to look for ones with the tails still on. That way, you've got built-in handles. Pretty nifty, huh?!"

Nutty Stuffed 'Shrooms

Serving Size: 2 mushrooms, Total Servings: 8

16 large mushrooms (about 1 pound)

1/2 small onion, minced

1/4 cup unsalted pistachios, coarsely chopped

1 tablespoon canola oil

1/3 cup crushed pretzels

2 tablespoons fat-free sour cream

2 tablespoons chopped fresh parsley

1/4 teaspoon black pepper

Dash hot pepper sauce (optional)

1 Preheat the oven to 350°F. Remove the mushroom stems from the caps; finely chop the stems.

2 In a large skillet, sauté the chopped mushroom stems, the onion, and the pistachios in the oil over medium heat for 2 to 4 minutes, or until the stems and onion are tender. Remove from the heat and stir in the remaining ingredients; mix well.

3 Stuff each mushroom cap and place on a large ungreased rimmed baking sheet. Bake for 20 to 25 minutes, or until the mushrooms are tender.

Good for You!

This recipe gives us a double dose of goodness, since mushrooms are low in fat yet loaded with fiber and protein, and pistachios contain mono-unsaturated fat, which helps fight cholesterol build-up.

Exchanges
1/2 Carbohydrate
1/2 Fat

Calories 69
 Calories from Fat . . . 35
Total Fat . . . . 4 g
 Saturated Fat . . . . . . 0.4 g
Cholesterol . . . . 0 mg
Sodium . . . . 45 mg
Total Carbohydrate . . . 7 g
 Dietary Fiber . . . . 1 g
 Sugars . . . . 2 g
Protein . . . . 3 g

Garlic Pita Crisps

Serving Size: 6 triangles, Total Servings: 16

6 6-inch whole-wheat pita breads

Nonstick vegetable spray

2 tablespoons garlic powder

1 Preheat the oven to 350°F. Cut each pita into 8 equal wedges. Separate each wedge into 2 pieces.

2 Coat both sides of the pita wedges lightly with nonstick vegetable spray and place in a single layer on large rimmed baking sheets; sprinkle with the garlic powder. Bake for 15 minutes, or until golden and crisp.

3 Allow the crisps to cool; serve immediately, or store in an airtight container until ready to use.

Exchanges
1 Starch

Calories 56
  Calories from Fat 5
Total Fat . . . . 1 g
  Saturated Fat . . . . 0 g
Cholesterol . . . . 0 mg
Sodium . . . . 49 mg
Total Carbohydrate . . 12 g
  Dietary Fiber . . . . 1 g
  Sugars . . . . 1 g
Protein . . . . 2 g

"Decisions, decisions! Try these crisps with Parmesan–Spinach Dip (page 15), Roasted Red Pepper Dip (page 16), or Garlic-Lover's Hummus (page 18). I love 'em all, so I rotate!"

Bistro Bruschetta

1/4 cup olive oil

1-1/4 teaspoons garlic powder

1 loaf (16 ounces) Italian or French bread, cut into 1-inch slices

8 plum tomatoes, seeded and chopped

1/4 cup chopped fresh basil

1/2 a small red onion, finely chopped

Salt to taste

1/4 teaspoon black pepper

1 Preheat the oven to 400°F. In a large bowl, combine the oil and garlic powder; mix well and set aside 2 tablespoons of the mixture.

2 Brush the tops of the bread slices with the remaining oil mixture and place on a baking sheet. Bake for 8 to 10 minutes, or until golden. Meanwhile, in the same large bowl, combine the remaining ingredients with the reserved oil mixture.

3 Spoon the tomato-onion mixture over the toasted bread slices and serve.

Exchanges
1-1/2 Starch
1/2 Fat

Calories 137
  Calories from Fat . . . 38
Total Fat . . . . 4 g
  Saturated Fat . . . . 1 g
Cholesterol . . . . 0 mg
Sodium . . . . 230 mg
Total Carbohydrate . . 21 g
  Dietary Fiber . . . . 1 g
  Sugars . . . . 1 g
Protein . . . . 4 g

"These Italian appe-teasers are hard to resist, and the best part is we can have 'em ready in about 10 minutes!"

Anytime Salads

Stacked Taco Salad

Serving Size: 1/12 recipe, Total Servings: 12

1 pound extra-lean ground beef

1 package (1-1/4 ounces) dry taco seasoning mix

1 medium head iceberg lettuce, chopped (about 8 cups)

3/4 cup (3 ounces) reduced-fat shredded Cheddar cheese

1 can (16 ounces) kidney beans, rinsed and drained

2 large tomatoes, diced (about 2 cups)

1 bag (8 ounces) baked tortilla chips, crushed

1 cup (8 ounces) sweet-and-spicy low-fat French salad dressing

1 In a medium skillet, brown the ground beef with the taco seasoning mix, stirring to break up the meat; drain and cool.

2 In a large glass trifle or other serving bowl, layer half of the lettuce, then half of the cheese, beans, ground beef, and tomatoes. Repeat the layers, then top with the crushed tortilla chips. Just before serving, drizzle with the dressing and toss to coat the ingredients well.

Exchanges

2 Starch
1 Vegetable
1 Lean Meat
1/2 Fat

Calories 230
  Calories from Fat . . . 62
Total Fat . . . . 7 g
  Saturated Fat . . . . . . 2.4 g
Cholesterol . . . . 28 mg
Sodium . . . . 643 mg
Total Carbohydrate . . 32 g
  Dietary Fiber . . . . 4 g
  Sugars . . . . 5 g
Protein . . . . 15 g

"Not only is this salad great tasting, but it's great looking, too! I suggest serving it in a trifle bowl or clear glass serving bowl so everybody can see all its colorful layers."

Fruit-full Tossed Chicken Salad

Serving Size: 1/4 recipe, Total Servings: 4

1 package (4 ounces) mixed baby greens

2 cups chunked cooked chicken breast

2 scallions, thinly sliced

1 cup sliced strawberries

1 can (15 ounces) no-sugar-added sliced peaches, drained with liquid reserved

3 tablespoons no-sugar-added peach preserves

1 tablespoon red wine vinegar

1 teaspoon yellow mustard

1/8 teaspoon ground red pepper

1 In a large salad bowl, combine the baby greens, chicken, scallions, strawberries, and peaches.

2 In a small bowl, combine 1/3 cup of the reserved peach liquid, the peach preserves, vinegar, mustard, and ground red pepper; mix well. Pour over the salad and toss well. Serve immediately.

Exchanges
3 Very Lean Meat
1-1/2 Fruit

Calories 202
  Calories from Fat . . . 25
Total Fat . . . . 3 g
  Saturated Fat . . . . 1 g
Cholesterol . . . . 60 mg
Sodium . . . . 84 mg
Total Carbohydrate . . 21 g
  Dietary Fiber . . . . 3 g
  Sugars . . . . 16 g
Protein . . . . 23 g

"Check out all these colorful ingredients. Fresh fruits and vegetables are full of natural sugars, so here we get to use that to our advantage! This main-dish salad can satisfy our sweet craving without all the guilt. Not a bad deal, huh?"

Green Bean and Tomato Toss

Serving Size: 1 cup, Total Servings: 6

1 pound fresh green beans, trimmed and cut in half

1-1/2 teaspoons salt, divided

4 large plum tomatoes, cut into chunks

1/4 cup chopped fresh basil

2 tablespoons extra-virgin olive oil

1 tablespoon fresh lemon juice

1 Place the green beans in a large saucepan. Add 1 teaspoon of the salt and enough water to cover the beans. Bring to a boil, cover, and cook for 6 to 8 minutes, or until tender; drain well.

2 Meanwhile, in a salad bowl, combine the tomatoes, basil, olive oil, lemon juice, and the remaining 1/2 teaspoon salt; mix well. Add the green beans and toss.

3 Serve at room temperature, or cover and chill until ready to serve.

Good for You!

Since veggies hold one of the keys to fighting certain diseases, let's not hold back! Join the attack ... and this colorful salad is a perfect start!

Exchanges
1 Vegetable
1 Fat

Calories 67
 Calories from Fat . . . 39
Total Fat . . . . 4 g
 Saturated Fat . . . . 1 g
Cholesterol . . . . 0 mg
Sodium . . . . 316 mg
Total Carbohydrate . . . 7 g
 Dietary Fiber . . . . 3 g
 Sugars . . . . 2 g
Protein . . . . 2 g

Dill 'n' Chill Shrimp

Serving Size: 1/4 recipe, Total Servings: 4

1 package (12 ounces) frozen cooked jumbo shrimp, thawed

1 small onion, thinly sliced

1 can (5 ounces) sliced water chestnuts, drained

1/3 cup reduced-fat Italian dressing

2 tablespoons chopped fresh dill

1 head romaine lettuce, chopped

2 medium tomatoes, quartered

1 In a medium bowl, combine the shrimp, onion, water chestnuts, Italian dressing, and dill; mix well. Cover and chill for 2 hours, or until well chilled.

2 Evenly divide the lettuce among 4 plates. Top with the shrimp mixture and garnish with the tomato wedges. Serve immediately.

Good for You!

Give that salt shaker a rest! Instead, do what we do in this recipe and get out the fresh herbs to add flavor and shake up your meals.

Exchanges
3 Very Lean Meat
2 Vegetable

Calories 147
  Calories from Fat . . . 18
Total Fat . . . . 2 g
  Saturated Fat . . . . 0 g
Cholesterol . . . . 165 mg
Sodium . . . . 504 mg
Total Carbohydrate . . 13 g
  Dietary Fiber . . . . 4 g
  Sugars . . . . 6 g
Protein . . . . 20 g

Mandarin Spinach Salad

Serving Size: 1/6 recipe, Total Servings: 6

1 can (11 ounces) mandarin oranges, drained

1/3 cup light Italian dressing

1 tablespoon poppy seeds (optional)

1 package (10 ounces) fresh spinach, trimmed

3 fresh oranges, peeled and sectioned

1 In a blender, combine the mandarin oranges and the Italian dressing. Blend until smooth. Stir in poppy seeds, if using.

2 In a large salad bowl, toss together the spinach, fresh orange sections, and half of the dressing mixture. Serve immediately.

Note

You're gonna end up with a double batch of this dressing, so keep it covered in the fridge and you'll be ready to go for another salad anytime in the next few weeks!

Exchanges
1 Fruit

Calories 51
 Calories from Fat 4
Total Fat . . . . 0 g
 Saturated Fat . . . . 0 g
Cholesterol . . . . 0 mg
Sodium . . . . 140 mg
Total Carbohydrate . . 11 g
 Dietary Fiber . . . . 3 g
 Sugars . . . . 7 g
Protein . . . . 2 g

Sesame Cabbage Salad

Serving Size: 1/12 recipe, Total Servings: 12

- **1** tablespoon peanut oil
- **1/4** cup sesame seeds
- **4** garlic cloves, minced
- **2** tablespoons soy sauce
- **2** tablespoons white vinegar
- **3** tablespoons sugar
- **1/4** cup canola oil
- **1** head Napa or Chinese cabbage, washed and cut into bite-sized pieces

1 In a medium saucepan, heat the peanut oil over medium heat. Add the sesame seeds and garlic, and sauté for 3 to 5 minutes, until the seeds are golden brown.

2 Reduce the heat to medium-low; add the soy sauce, vinegar, sugar, and canola oil, and cook for 2 more minutes.

3 Place the cabbage in a large bowl and pour the warm dressing over it, tossing to coat completely. Serve immediately (see below).

Exchanges
1/2 Starch
1 Fat

Calories	89
Calories from Fat	67
Total Fat	7 g
Saturated Fat	1 g
Cholesterol	0 mg
Sodium	175 mg
Total Carbohydrate	5 g
Dietary Fiber	1 g
Sugars	4 g
Protein	1 g

"This dressing is great warm, so we originally planned on serving this as a warm salad, but we found out that the salad's great cold, too, so go ahead and enjoy it either way . . . or both!"

Zippy Cucumber Crunch

Serving Size: 1/2 cup, Total Servings: 8

2 large cucumbers, peeled and sliced

1 teaspoon salt

3 cups ice water

4 scallions, thinly sliced

1/2 small green bell pepper, chopped

1/4 cup reduced-fat sour cream

1 tablespoon white vinegar

1 tablespoon sugar

1/8 teaspoon black pepper

1 In a large bowl, combine the cucumbers, salt, and ice water. Cover and chill for 1 hour, then drain and return the cucumbers to the bowl.

2 Add the remaining ingredients and mix until well combined. Cover and chill for at least 2 hours before serving.

Did You Know . . .

that soaking cucumber slices in salted ice water gives them extra crunch?

Exchanges
1 Vegetable

Calories 30
 Calories from Fat 7
Total Fat . . . . 1 g
 Saturated Fat . . . . 0 g
Cholesterol . . . . 2 mg
Sodium . . . . 104 mg
Total Carbohydrate . . . 5 g
 Dietary Fiber . . . . 1 g
 Sugars . . . . 4 g
Protein . . . . 1 g

Picture-Perfect Tomato Stack

Serving Size: 1 tomato, Total Servings: 4

4 large ripe tomatoes

1 package (4 ounces) mixed baby greens

1/2 cup balsamic vinaigrette dressing, divided

1/4 cup crumbled blue cheese

1 Cut a very thin slice from the bottom of each tomato so it stands up; discard the slices or set aside for another use. Cut each tomato horizontally into 5 slices, keeping the slices together.

2 In a small bowl, combine the baby greens, 1/4 cup of the dressing, and the blue cheese; toss well. Place the bottom tomato slices on a serving dish. Using 1/4 of the salad mixture, equally top the tomato slices.

3 Repeat the layers three more times, ending with the top tomato slices. Drizzle with the remaining 1/4 cup dressing, then serve.

Exchanges
1/2 Carbohydrate
2 Vegetable

Calories 88	
Calories from Fat . . . 24	
Total Fat . . . . 3 g	
Saturated Fat . . . . 1 g	
Cholesterol . . . . 5 mg	
Sodium . . . . 120 mg	
Total Carbohydrate . . 16 g	
Dietary Fiber . . . . 2 g	
Sugars . . . . 10 g	
Protein . . . . 3 g	

"Say 'cheese,' because you're gonna want to take a picture of this eye-catching dish! Plus, for a change of pace, why not add some sliced cooked chicken or shrimp to the baby greens (before layering in the tomatoes) to make it even heartier. A little extra blue cheese on top can't hurt, either!"

Tokyo Toss

Serving Size: 1/6 recipe, Total Servings: 6

1/4 cup peanut oil

2 tablespoons white vinegar

2 tablespoons water

1 tablespoon soy sauce

1 teaspoon lemon juice

1 tablespoon ketchup

1 teaspoon ground ginger

1 teaspoon sugar

1/4 teaspoon black pepper

1/4 cup chopped onions

1 package (10 ounces) fresh spinach, trimmed

1 package (8 ounces) fresh sliced mushrooms

1 In a blender or food processor, combine all the ingredients except the spinach and mushrooms; blend until smooth.

2 In a large salad bowl, combine the spinach, mushrooms, and dressing mixture; toss well and serve.

Exchanges
1 Vegetable
2 Fat

Calories 107
   Calories from Fat . . . 84
Total Fat . . . . 9 g
   Saturated Fat . . . . 2 g
Cholesterol . . . . 0 mg
Sodium . . . . 239 mg
Total Carbohydrate . . . 5 g
   Dietary Fiber . . . . 2 g
   Sugars . . . . 2 g
Protein . . . . 2 g

"Instead of eating this salad with a fork, why not get into the Asian theme by using chopsticks? And if you have no success, it's okay to get out the forks—at least you'll have had fun trying!"

Deli Salad Kabob

Serving Size: 1 skewer, Total servings: 6

4 slices (1/4 pound) low-sodium deli turkey

4 slices (1/4 pound) low-sodium deli ham

4 slices (2 ounces) reduced-fat Swiss or yellow Cheddar cheese

4 slices (1/4 pound) deli roast beef

1 small head iceberg lettuce, cut into 12 chunks

1 large tomato, cut into 12 chunks

6 10-inch skewers

1 Place the turkey slices on a work surface and top each with a slice of ham, then cheese, then roast beef. Starting at the narrow end, tightly roll up jelly-roll style and slice each roll into three equal pieces.

2 Alternately thread each skewer with two each of the roll-up pieces, lettuce chunks, and tomato chunks. Serve immediately, or cover and chill until ready to serve. Just before serving, drizzle lightly with your favorite salad dressing.

Exchanges
1 Vegetable
2 Very Lean Meat

Calories 109	
Calories from Fat . . . 24	
Total Fat . . . . 3 g	
Saturated Fat . . . . . . 1.2 g	
Cholesterol . . . . 36 mg	
Sodium . . . . 373 mg	
Total Carbohydrate . . . 3 g	
Dietary Fiber . . . . 1 g	
Sugars . . . . 2 g	
Protein . . . . 17 g	

"When is a sandwich not a sandwich? When it's on a stick, that's when! This breadless deli favorite is sure to become a favorite of yours, and everyone else's, too, since so many of us are watching our carbs these days."

Waldorf Salad

2 tablespoons lemon juice

1/2 cup light mayonnaise

2 celery stalks, chopped

1 cup red seedless grapes, cut in half

4 MacIntosh apples, cored and cut into 1-inch chunks

2 tablespoons chopped walnuts

1 In a large bowl, whisk together the lemon juice and mayonnaise until well combined.

2 Add the remaining ingredients except the walnuts and toss to coat. Cover and chill for at least 1 hour before serving.

3 Just before serving, sprinkle chopped walnuts over the top.

Exchanges
1 Fruit
1 Fat

Calories 119
  Calories from Fat . . . 58
Total Fat . . . . 6 g
  Saturated Fat . . . . 1 g
Cholesterol . . . . 5 mg
Sodium . . . . 130 mg
Total Carbohydrate . . 16 g
  Dietary Fiber . . . . 2 g
  Sugars . . . . 12 g
Protein . . . . 1 g

"Fresh fruit was always an important part of my meal plan—especially during the days of my early pageant competitions, before I was diagnosed with diabetes. Now that I'm watching my meal plan for different reasons, recipes like this one are a real treat because they let me enjoy fresh fruit in interesting combinations."

Scrumptious Soups

Roma Tomato Bisque

Serving Size: 1 cup, Total Servings: 7

2 cans (28 ounces each) crushed tomatoes

1 tablespoon sugar

1 tablespoon chopped fresh basil or 1 teaspoon dried basil

1/2 teaspoon garlic powder

1 teaspoon black pepper

1 can (12 ounces) low-fat evaporated milk

1 In a soup pot, combine the tomatoes, sugar, basil, garlic powder, and pepper; bring to a boil over medium-high heat, stirring occasionally.

2 Reduce the heat to low and slowly stir in the evaporated milk. Simmer for 4 to 5 minutes, or until heated through; do not allow to boil.

Finishing Touch

A leaf or sprig of fresh basil on a dollop of fat-free sour cream looks great topping each serving!

Exchanges
2 Carbohydrate

Calories 143
  Calories from Fat 4
Total Fat . . . . 0 g
  Saturated Fat . . . . 0 g
Cholesterol . . . . 0 mg
Sodium . . . . 700 mg
Total Carbohydrate . . 27 g
  Dietary Fiber . . . . 5 g
  Sugars . . . . 18 g
Protein . . . . 8 g

Round-'Em-Up Bean Soup

Serving Size: 1 cup, Total Servings: 11

1 teaspoon olive oil

1 pound hot Italian turkey sausage, casings removed (see Note)

1 small onion, chopped

2 garlic cloves, minced

3 cans (15-1/2 ounces each) Great Northern beans, undrained

2 cans (14-1/2 ounces each) ready-to-use reduced-sodium chicken broth

1 can (14-1/2 ounces) diced tomatoes, undrained

1 teaspoon dried basil

1/2 teaspoon black pepper

1. In a large soup pot, heat the oil over medium-high heat. Add the sausage, onion, and garlic, and cook for 5 to 6 minutes, or until no pink remains in the sausage, stirring frequently to break it up.

2. Add the remaining ingredients and bring to a boil. Reduce the heat to medium-low and simmer, uncovered, for 30 minutes.

Exchanges
2 Starch
2 Very Lean Meat

Calories 226
  Calories from Fat . . . 39
Total Fat . . . . 4 g
  Saturated Fat . . . . 2 g
Cholesterol . . . . 32 mg
Sodium . . . . 958 mg
Total Carbohydrate . . 30 g
  Dietary Fiber . . . . 6 g
  Sugars . . . . 5 g
Protein . . . . 17 g

Note

Some like it hot, and some don't, so if you want to turn down the heat in this recipe, simply use a mild-flavored sausage.

Bistro Onion Soup

4 medium onions, thinly sliced

2 cans (14-1/2 ounces each) ready-to-use beef broth

2 cups water

1/4 cup dry red wine

1/2 teaspoon black pepper

1/4 cup grated Parmesan cheese

6 slices French bread, toasted

1 Coat a soup pot with nonstick cooking spray. Add the onions and sauté over medium heat for 12 to 15 minutes, or until browned.

2 Add the broth, water, wine, and pepper; mix well and bring to a boil. Reduce the heat to low and simmer for 10 minutes. Stir in the cheese and simmer for 5 to 10 minutes, or until thoroughly blended.

3 Ladle into bowls and top each with a slice of toasted French bread.

Exchanges
1-1/2 Starch
1 Vegetable
1/2 Fat

Calories 171
   Calories from Fat . . . 36
Total Fat . . . . 4 g
   Saturated Fat . . . . 1 g
Cholesterol . . . . 8 mg
Sodium . . . . 945 mg
Total Carbohydrate . . 26 g
   Dietary Fiber . . . . 3 g
   Sugars . . . . 8 g
Protein . . . . 8 g

"If you want that traditional cheesy topping, top each slice of French bread with a slice of low-fat provolone or mozzarella cheese and broil or toast in a toaster oven until the cheese melts. Then place each one carefully over a bowl of soup."

Mushroom Barley Soup

6 cups water

2 cans (10-1/2 ounces each) condensed beef broth

1 pound beef top round, cut into 1/2-inch chunks

2 large onions, chopped

1/2 pound sliced fresh mushrooms

4 medium carrots, peeled and sliced

1 can (14-1/2 ounces) diced tomatoes, drained

3/4 teaspoon black pepper

1 cup quick-cooking pearl barley

1 In a soup pot, combine all the ingredients except the barley; cover and bring to a boil over high heat. Reduce the heat to low and simmer, covered, for 20 minutes, stirring occasionally.

2 Add the barley and simmer for 15 to 20 more minutes, or until the barley is tender.

Exchanges

1/2 Starch
1 Very Lean Meat
1 Vegetable

Calories 98
  Calories from Fat . . . 12
Total Fat . . . . 1 g
  Saturated Fat . . . . 0 g
Cholesterol . . . . 16 mg
Sodium . . . . 213 mg
Total Carbohydrate . . 14 g
  Dietary Fiber . . . . 2 g
  Sugars . . . . 4 g
Protein . . . . 9 g

"Jewish Penicillin"
(a.k.a. Homemade Chicken Soup)

Serving Size: 1 cup, Total Servings: 10

1 3-pound chicken, cut into 8 pieces

8 cups cold water

4 carrots, cut into 1-inch chunks

3 celery stalks, cut into 1-inch chunks

2 medium onions, cut into 1-inch chunks

1 teaspoon salt

1-1/2 teaspoons black pepper

1 In a soup pot, bring all the ingredients to a boil over high heat. Reduce the heat to low, cover, and simmer for 2-1/2 to 3 hours, or until the chicken is falling off the bones.

2 Using tongs, remove the chicken from the soup and allow it to cool slightly before removing and discarding its bones and skin; cut the chicken into small pieces, and return those to the soup pot.

Exchanges
2 Very Lean Meat
1 Vegetable

Calories 113	
Calories from Fat . . . 30	
Total Fat . . . . 3 g	
Saturated Fat . . . . 1 g	
Cholesterol . . . . 39 mg	
Sodium . . . . 297 mg	
Total Carbohydrate . . . 7 g	
Dietary Fiber . . . . 2 g	
Sugars . . . . 4 g	
Protein . . . . 14 g	

"Be a believer! Many doctors claim that chicken soup may actually help cure the common cold. And even when we don't have a cold, we can enjoy the soup as above, or lighten it up by skimming off and discarding any fat that rises to the top after the soup cools."

Manhattan Clam Chowder

2 slices raw bacon, minced

2 ribs celery, chopped

2 medium carrots, chopped

1 large onion, chopped

3 medium potatoes, peeled and diced

2 cans (14-1/2 ounces each) diced tomatoes, undrained

2 cans (10 ounces each) baby clams, undrained

2 bottles (8 ounces each) clam juice

1 teaspoon dried thyme

1 In a soup pot, cook the bacon for 3 to 5 minutes over medium-high heat, until crisp. Add the celery, carrots, and onion, and sauté for 5 to 7 minutes, or until the onion is tender, stirring frequently.

2 Add the remaining ingredients, cover, and bring to a boil. Reduce the heat to low and simmer, covered, for 45 to 55 minutes, or until the potatoes are very tender.

Exchanges
1 Starch
1 Lean Meat

Calories	133
Calories from Fat . . .	31
Total Fat	3 g
Saturated Fat	1 g
Cholesterol	22 mg
Sodium	407 mg
Total Carbohydrate . .	17 g
Dietary Fiber	3 g
Sugars	7 g
Protein	9 g

"Canned soups are generally loaded with sodium, so what better reason do we need to give this scratch version a spin in our own kitchens?!"

Bayside Cioppino

1/2 pound fresh mushrooms, sliced

2 medium onions, thinly sliced

4 garlic cloves, minced

1 can (28 ounces) whole tomatoes, undrained and quartered

1/2 cup dry white wine

2 tablespoons chopped fresh basil

3/4 teaspoon black pepper

1 pound cod fillets, cut into 2-inch chunks

1/2 pound bay scallops

1/2 pound large shrimp, peeled and deveined, with tails left on

1 Spray a 6-quart soup pot with nonstick cooking spray and heat over high heat. Add the mushrooms, onions, and garlic, and cook for 4 to 6 minutes, or until the vegetables are tender, stirring often. Stir in the tomatoes, wine, basil, and pepper and bring to a boil.

2 Reduce the heat to low, cover, and simmer for 20 minutes. Uncover, increase the heat to high, and bring to a boil.

3 Add the fish and cook for 5 minutes. Add the scallops and shrimp and cook for 3 minutes, or until the fish flakes easily with a fork and the shrimp are pink and cooked through, stirring occasionally.

Did You Know ...

that we used to think people with diabetes had to avoid alcohol? Now we know that as long as you account for the extra carbohydrate in your total for the day, and consume occasional and moderate quantities, you should be fine! (Of course, always check with your physician and/or dietitian first.)

Exchanges

3 Very Lean Meat
2 Vegetable

Calories 144
   Calories from Fat . . . 13
Total Fat . . . . 1 g
   Saturated Fat . . . . 0 g
Cholesterol . . . . 76 mg
Sodium . . . . 267 mg
Total Carbohydrate . . 10 g
   Dietary Fiber . . . . 2 g
   Sugars . . . . 6 g
Protein . . . . 22 g

Italian Veggie Soup

Serving Size: 1 cup, Total Servings: 14

2 cups water

2 cans (14-1/2 ounces each) ready-to-use beef broth

1 can (15 ounces) red kidney beans

1 can (14 to 16 ounces) cannellini (white kidney) beans

1 can (28 ounces) crushed tomatoes

1 package (10 ounces) frozen chopped spinach

1 small onion, chopped

1 package (10 ounces) frozen mixed vegetables

1 teaspoon garlic powder

1/2 teaspoon black pepper

1 cup uncooked elbow macaroni

1 In a soup pot, combine all the ingredients except the macaroni. Bring to a boil over high heat then add the macaroni.

2 Reduce the heat to low and simmer for 20 to 30 minutes, or until the macaroni is tender.

Exchanges
1 Starch
2 Vegetable

Calories 137
  Calories from Fat 7
Total Fat . . . . 1 g
  Saturated Fat . . . . 0 g
Cholesterol . . . . 1 mg
Sodium . . . . 643 mg
Total Carbohydrate . . 26 g
  Dietary Fiber . . . . 5 g
  Sugars . . . . 6 g
Protein . . . . 8 g

"Get a big flavor boost from Parmesan cheese. Yup, with stronger-flavored cheeses, a little goes a long way, so try sprinkling a bit of grated Parmesan over the top of this soup— and other foods—just before serving."

Icy-Hot Gazpacho

Serving Size: 1 cup, Total Servings: 10

1 can (14-1/2 ounces) diced tomatoes, drained

1 can (46 ounces) no-salt-added tomato juice

1 large cucumber, peeled, seeded, and diced

1 medium-sized green bell pepper, diced

5 scallions, thinly sliced

3 garlic cloves, minced

1/3 cup white vinegar

1 tablespoon olive oil

2 teaspoons Worcestershire sauce

1/2 teaspoon hot pepper sauce

1 In a large bowl, combine all the ingredients; mix well.

2 Cover and chill for at least 4 hours before serving.

Finishing Touch

To give this soup a little extra flair, add a swirl of low-fat sour cream to each serving, and garnish that with a sprig of fresh dill. It's so easy to make it look fancy!

Exchanges
2 Vegetable

Calories 55
Calories from Fat . . . 13
Total Fat . . . . 1 g
Saturated Fat . . . . 0 g
Cholesterol . . . . 0 mg
Sodium . . . . 99 mg
Total Carbohydrate . . 11 g
Dietary Fiber . . . . 2 g
Sugars . . . . 7 g
Protein . . . . 2 g

Thick 'n' Creamy Mushroom Soup

1 pound fresh sliced mushrooms

2 cans (14-1/2 ounces each) ready-to-use reduced-sodium chicken broth

1/2 teaspoon onion powder

1/8 teaspoon black pepper

1 cup low-fat milk

5 tablespoons all-purpose flour

1/4 teaspoon browning and seasoning sauce

1 Coat a soup pot with nonstick cooking spray. Add the mushrooms and sauté over high heat for 4 to 5 minutes, or until soft, stirring frequently.

2 Add the chicken broth, onion powder, and pepper; bring to a boil, then reduce the heat to medium-low.

3 In a small bowl, mix the milk and flour until smooth. Gradually add to the soup, stirring constantly. Stir in the browning and seasoning sauce and simmer for 5 more minutes, or until thickened.

Exchanges
1 Carbohydrate

Calories 89
Calories from Fat 9
Total Fat . . . . 1 g
Saturated Fat . . . . 0 g
Cholesterol . . . . 2 mg
Sodium . . . . 413 mg
Total Carbohydrate . . 14 g
Dietary Fiber . . . . 1 g
Sugars . . . . 4 g
Protein . . . . 7 g

"This soup is ready in a snap! When it's one that goes from stove to table in less than 30 minutes, how can you NOT find the time to give it a try?"

New England Clam Chowder

Serving Size: 1 cup, Total Servings: 6

1 small onion, chopped

2 cans (6-1/2 ounces each) chopped clams, undrained

1 bottle (8 ounces) clam juice

1 can (16 ounces) ready-to-use reduced-sodium chicken broth

1 large potato, peeled and diced

1/4 teaspoon black pepper

1/4 cup cornstarch

1 can (12 ounces) low-fat evaporated milk, divided

1/4 cup chopped fresh parsley

1 teaspoon dried thyme

1 In a soup pot, combine the onion, clams in their juice, clam juice, chicken broth, potato, and pepper; cover and bring to a boil over high heat. Cook, covered, for 12 to 15 minutes, until the potatoes are tender.

2 In a small bowl, dissolve the cornstarch in 1/2 cup evaporated milk; add to the soup.

3 Add the remaining evaporated milk, the parsley, and thyme; cook for 5 minutes, or until thickened, stirring frequently.

Exchanges
1-1/2 Carbohydrate
1 Very Lean Meat

Calories	158	
Calories from Fat	 8	
Total Fat	1	g
Saturated Fat	0	g
Cholesterol	25	mg
Sodium	422	mg
Total Carbohydrate . .	21	g
Dietary Fiber	1	g
Sugars	9	g
Protein	16	g

"Ahoy there! This rich and chunky 'chowda' reminds me of foggy New England harbors and the fishing fleet coming home with their catch. With its hearty broth, it's still an option for us when we use low-fat and low-sodium ingredients to make a healthier alternative to the original version."

Mexican Tortilla Soup

Serving Size: 1 cup, Total Servings: 8

1 tablespoon vegetable oil

1 pound boneless, skinless chicken breast, cut into 1/2-inch chunks

1 red bell pepper, coarsely chopped

3 garlic cloves, minced

3 cans (14-1/2 ounces each) ready-to-use reduced-sodium chicken broth

1 package (10 ounces) frozen whole kernel corn

1/2 cup salsa

1/4 cup chopped fresh cilantro

1 cup broken-up baked tortilla chips

1 In a soup pot, heat the oil over medium heat. Add the chicken, bell pepper, and garlic, and cook for about 3 minutes, or until the chicken is browned on the outside, stirring frequently.

2 Stir in the chicken broth, corn, and salsa; bring to a boil. Reduce the heat to low, cover, and simmer for 5 minutes, or until the chicken is no longer pink.

3 Stir in the cilantro, ladle into bowls, and serve topped with the tortilla chips.

Exchanges
1 Starch
2 Very Lean Meat

Calories 149
   Calories from Fat . . . 32
Total Fat . . . . 4 g
   Saturated Fat . . . . 0 g
Cholesterol . . . . 34 mg
Sodium . . . . 417 mg
Total Carbohydrate . . 13 g
   Dietary Fiber . . . . 2 g
   Sugars . . . . 3 g
Protein . . . . 16 g

""Doesn't this recipe sound great? Well, it looks great, too—just take a peek at the finished dish in Photo Insert E."

Lip-Smackin' Poultry

Crustless Chicken Potpie

Serving Size: 1/8 recipe, Total Servings: 8

1 can (10-3/4 ounces) 98% fat-free, lower-sodium condensed cream of chicken soup

1/4 cup fat-free milk

3 cups cubed, cooked chicken breast

1 package (16 ounces) frozen peas and carrots, thawed and drained

1/2 teaspoon black pepper

corn
1 green red orange or Red bell peppers chopped

1. Preheat the oven to 425°F. In a large bowl, combine the soup, milk, chicken, and peas and carrots; mix well.

2. Pour the mixture into a 9-inch deep-dish pie plate. Place pie on a rimmed baking sheet and bake for 25 to 30 minutes, or until heated through. Spoon into bowls and serve.

Exchanges
1 Carbohydrate
2 Very Lean Meat

Calories 159	
Calories from Fat . . . 28	
Total Fat . . . . 3 g	
Saturated Fat . . . . 1 g	
Cholesterol . . . . 49 mg	
Sodium . . . . 263 mg	
Total Carbohydrate . . 11 g	
Dietary Fiber . . . . 2 g	
Sugars . . . . 4 g	
Protein . . . . 19 g	

"What's missing from this pie? The crust . . . and a lot of the fat! But it still has all the goodness of a potpie, so give it a try."

Garlic Roasted Chicken

Serving Size: 1 breast half, Total Servings: 4

4 bone-in chicken breast halves (about 8 ounces each), skin removed

2 tablespoons olive oil

1/2 teaspoon dried oregano

1 tablespoon chopped fresh basil

1/4 teaspoon salt

1/2 teaspoon black pepper

10 garlic cloves, sliced

1 Preheat the oven to 350°F. Place the chicken in a 9" × 13" baking dish; set aside.

2 In a small bowl, combine the oil, oregano, basil, salt, and pepper; mix well and brush over the chicken. Sprinkle the garlic over the chicken.

3 Bake for 50 to 60 minutes, or until the chicken is golden outside and no longer pink inside, turning occasionally.

Good for You!

Ah, garlic! Just a few cloves can make a dish go from flat to fantastic. And with a little experimenting, you can find creative ways to perk up otherwise plain meals with herbs and spices—which means diabetic meals need never be blah again!

Exchanges
5 Lean Meat

Calories 280
  Calories from Fat . . . 96
Total Fat . . . . 11 g
  Saturated Fat . . . . 3 g
Cholesterol . . . . 110 mg
Sodium . . . . 244 mg
Total Carbohydrate . . . 3 g
  Dietary Fiber . . . . 0 g
  Sugars . . . . 2 g
Protein . . . . 41 g

Sizzlin' Chicken

Serving Size: 1 rollup, Total Servings: 6

2 tablespoons canola oil, divided

2 large onions, each cut into 8 wedges

2 large bell peppers (1 red, 1 green), cut into 1/2-inch strips

1 pound boneless, skinless chicken breasts, cut into 1/4-inch strips

2 teaspoons garlic powder

1/4 teaspoon salt

1/2 teaspoon black pepper

Juice of 1 lime

6 8-inch tortillas

1 Heat 1 tablespoon oil in a large skillet over medium-high heat. Add the onions and bell peppers and sauté for 10 to 12 minutes, or until the onions are lightly browned; remove to a bowl and set aside.

2 Heat the remaining 1 tablespoon oil in the skillet and add the chicken, garlic powder, salt, and black pepper. Sauté for 5 to 6 minutes, or until no pink remains in the chicken.

3 Return the vegetables to the skillet and cook for 3 to 5 minutes, stirring occasionally. Pour the lime juice over the chicken and vegetables; mix well. Divide the chicken mixture equally among the tortillas and serve (see Finishing Touch below).

Exchanges
2 Starch
2 Lean Meat
2 Vegetable
1/2 Fat

Calories 334
Calories from Fat . . . 93
Total Fat . . . . 10 g
Saturated Fat . . . . 1 g
Cholesterol . . . . 46 mg
Sodium . . . . 375 mg
Total Carbohydrate . . 38 g
Dietary Fiber . . . . 4 g
Sugars . . . . 5 g
Protein . . . . 22 g

Finishing Touch

Know what's good rolled in with these? Shredded cheese, chopped tomatoes, and low-fat sour cream. Just don't forget: Moderation is key.

Sweet-and-Sour Chicken

2 tablespoons canola oil

2 pounds boneless, skinless chicken breast, cut into thin strips

1 can (20 ounces) pineapple chunks in heavy syrup, drained and liquid reserved

1 can (8 ounces) sliced water chestnuts, drained

1 cup fresh broccoli florets

1 medium-sized red bell pepper, cut into 3/4-inch chunks

2 tablespoons light soy sauce

1 tablespoon white vinegar

1 tablespoon ketchup

2 tablespoons cornstarch

2 tablespoons sugar

1 cup fresh snow peas, trimmed

1 Heat the oil in a large skillet or wok over high heat. Add the chicken and stir-fry for 4 to 5 minutes, or until no pink remains.

2 Add the pineapple chunks, water chestnuts, broccoli, and bell pepper. Stir-fry for 3 to 4 minutes, or until the vegetables are crisp-tender.

3 In a small bowl, combine the reserved pineapple liquid, the soy sauce, vinegar, ketchup, cornstarch, and sugar; mix well. Stir into the skillet and cook for 3 minutes. Add the snow peas and cook for 1 minute, or until the sauce thickens. Serve immediately.

Exchanges

1-1/2 Carbohydrate
3 Very Lean Meat
1 Vegetable
1 Fat

Calories 265
  Calories from Fat . . . 58
Total Fat . . . . 6 g
Saturated Fat . . . . 1 g
Cholesterol . . . . 68 mg
Sodium . . . . 245 mg
Total Carbohydrate . . 25 g
  Dietary Fiber . . . . 2 g
  Sugars . . . . 19 g
Protein . . . . 26 g

Johnsons' Pasta-Rama

Serving Size: 2 cups, Total Servings: 8

1 pound tri-colored twist pasta

1 pound lean ground turkey breast

1 jar (26 ounces) spaghetti sauce

1 medium onion, chopped

3 garlic cloves, minced

2 carrots, thinly sliced

2 medium-sized yellow squash, cut into 1/2-inch chunks

1 large zucchini, cut into 1/2-inch chunks

1 large green bell pepper, chopped

1/2 pound sliced mushrooms

1. Cook the pasta according to the package directions, omitting the salt; drain.

2. Meanwhile, in a soup pot, brown the turkey over high heat, stirring constantly. Add the remaining ingredients and reduce the heat to medium-low; cover and cook for 20 to 30 minutes, or until the vegetables are tender, stirring occasionally.

3. Add the pasta to the pot; mix well and cook until heated through. Serve immediately.

Exchanges
4-1/2 Carbohydrate
2 Very Lean Meat

Calories 431
  Calories from Fat . . . 50
Total Fat . . . . 6 g
  Saturated Fat . . . . 2 g
Cholesterol . . . . 39 mg
Sodium . . . . 535 mg
Total Carbohydrate . . 71 g
  Dietary Fiber . . . . 6 g
  Sugars . . . . 19 g
Protein . . . . 25 g

"This is one of my favorite meals. It is quick, easy, and so yummy! What a great dish to use for big family gatherings. Get everyone to pitch in—it adds to the fun!"

Chicken Cacciatore

Serving Size: 1 to 2 pieces, Total Servings: 5

1 large onion

1 tablespoon olive oil

1 package (8 ounces) sliced mushrooms

2 bell peppers (1 red, 1 green), thinly sliced

1 chicken (3 pounds), cut into 8 pieces and skin removed

1 jar (26 ounces) light spaghetti sauce

1/2 cup water

1 Cut the onion in half, then into 1/4-inch slices. In a large pot, heat the olive oil over medium-high heat. Sauté the onion, mushrooms, and bell peppers for 3 to 4 minutes, or just until tender. Remove the vegetables to a medium bowl, leaving any remaining liquid in the pot.

2 In the same pot, sauté the chicken pieces for 4 to 5 minutes per side, or until golden. Return the sautéed vegetables to the pot. Add the spaghetti sauce and water; mix well.

3 Reduce the heat to medium-low, cover, and cook for 35 to 40 minutes, or until the chicken is tender and cooked through.

Exchanges
1 Carbohydrate
4 Very Lean Meat
1 Vegetable
1 Fat

Calories 286	
Calories from Fat . . . 84	
Total Fat . . . . 9 g	
Saturated Fat . . . . 2 g	
Cholesterol . . . . 77 mg	
Sodium . . . . 809 mg	
Total Carbohydrate . . 21 g	
Dietary Fiber . . . . 6 g	
Sugars . . . . 13 g	
Protein . . . . 30 g	

Good for You!

Take a walk! Besides cutting down on portion sizes, becoming more active may be all you need to do to control weight and blood sugar levels. The best time to exercise is generally about 30 to 60 minutes after breakfast or dinner, but be sure to consult your diabetes care team to find out what's best for you. And, you know, EVERYONE can benefit from leading this type of lifestyle.

Barbecue-Glazed Drumsticks

Serving Size: 2 drumsticks, Total Servings: 4

1/2 cup apple cider vinegar

1/3 cup yellow mustard

2 tablespoons light brown sugar

1 tablespoon butter

1/2 teaspoon light soy sauce

1/2 teaspoon chili powder

1/8 teaspoon ground red pepper

1/2 teaspoon black pepper

8 drumsticks, skin removed

1 Preheat the oven to 375°F. Coat an 8-inch square baking dish with nonstick cooking spray.

2 In a medium saucepan, combine all the ingredients except the drumsticks over medium heat. Bring to a boil and allow to boil for 5 minutes, or until the sauce thickens, stirring constantly.

3 Place the drumsticks in the baking dish and pour the sauce mixture over them, coating completely. Bake for 40 to 45 minutes, or until the chicken is no longer pink and the juices run clear.

Exchanges

1 Carbohydrate
3 Lean Meat
1/2 Fat

Calories	264
Calories from Fat	97
Total Fat	11 g
Saturated Fat	3 g
Cholesterol	88 mg
Sodium	508 mg
Total Carbohydrate	16 g
Dietary Fiber	4 g
Sugars	11 g
Protein	28 g

"Don't think you're gonna get all heated up standing over the barbecue grill—uh uh! These guys do their cooking in the oven. Although there is a bit of sugar in this dish, your dietitian should be able to help you work foods with small amounts of sugar into your meal plan; don't be afraid to ask!"

Soda-Can Chicken

Serving Size: 1 to 2 pieces, Total Servings: 5

1/2 cup barbecue sauce

1 can (12 ounces) diet lemon-lime soda, half full

1 tablespoon dried basil

2 teaspoons paprika

1/2 teaspoon onion powder

1/4 teaspoon garlic powder

1/4 teaspoon salt

1/4 teaspoon black pepper

1 whole chicken (3-1/2 pounds), skin removed

1 Remove top oven rack. Preheat the oven to 350°F. Add the barbecue sauce to the half-full can of soda. In a small bowl, combine the basil, paprika, onion powder, garlic powder, salt, and pepper; mix well and rub evenly over the chicken.

2 Place the cavity of the chicken over the soda can so that the chicken is sitting vertically on the can, then place the can on a rimmed baking sheet and bake on bottom oven rack for 1-1/2 to 1-3/4 hours, or until no pink remains and the juices run clear.

3 Cut the chicken into serving-sized pieces and carefully pour the remaining sauce from the can over the chicken.

Exchanges
5 Very Lean Meat
1 Fat

Calories	218
Calories from Fat	73
Total Fat	8 g
Saturated Fat	2 g
Cholesterol	90 mg
Sodium	409 mg
Total Carbohydrate	4 g
Dietary Fiber	1 g
Sugars	3 g
Protein	30 g

Note

This sure is a fun way to cook chicken, but be careful—the soda can is VERY HOT when it comes out of the oven, so use oven mitts when handling it.

Balsamic Chicken

Serving Size: 1 breast half, Total Servings: 4

1/4 cup balsamic vinegar

2 tablespoons olive oil

1/2 teaspoon garlic powder

1/4 teaspoon salt

1/4 teaspoon black pepper

4 boneless, skinless chicken breast halves

1 Combine all the ingredients in a large resealable plastic storage bag; mix well. Seal and marinate in the refrigerator for 30 minutes.

2 Heat a grill pan over medium heat until hot. Place the chicken on the pan, discarding excess marinade, and cook for 6 to 10 minutes per side, or until no pink remains and the juices run clear.

Exchanges
5 Very Lean Meat
1/2 Fat

Calories 199	
Calories from Fat . . . 59	
Total Fat . . . . 7 g	
Saturated Fat . . . . 2 g	
Cholesterol . . . . 85 mg	
Sodium . . . . 144 mg	
Total Carbohydrate . . . 2 g	
Dietary Fiber . . . . 0 g	
Sugars . . . . 1 g	
Protein . . . . 31 g	

"When I found out I had diabetes, I thought bland foods would be all I'd be able to eat. Boy, was I wrong! Just try this tangy chicken. It cooks quickly in a skillet or on a grill. And when it's teamed with steamed or grilled veggies, we can all feel like we're splurging!"

Skillet Greek Chicken

Serving Size: 1 to 2 pieces, Total Servings: 5

2 tablespoons olive oil

3 tablespoons lemon juice, divided

2 tablespoons chopped fresh parsley, divided

2 teaspoons dried oregano

1/4 teaspoon black pepper

1 chicken (3 pounds), cut into 8 pieces and skin removed

1/2 cup crumbled fat-free feta cheese

1 In a medium bowl, combine the olive oil, 2 tablespoons lemon juice, 1 tablespoon parsley, the oregano, and pepper; mix well. Add the chicken and turn to coat evenly.

2 Heat a large skillet over high heat and brown the chicken for 5 to 6 minutes per side; then reduce the heat to low, cover, and simmer for 10 minutes.

3 Add the remaining 1 tablespoon each of lemon juice and parsley and the feta cheese; cover and simmer for 5 minutes, or until the cheese softens and the chicken is no longer pink.

Exchanges
4 Lean Meat

Calories	234
Calories from Fat	108
Total Fat	12 g
Saturated Fat	2.5 g
Cholesterol	78 mg
Sodium	316 mg
Total Carbohydrate	2 g
Dietary Fiber	0 g
Sugars	1 g
Protein	29 g

"This quick chicken dish is only on the stove for 20 minutes, so you'll be feasting in a snap! The feta cheese is really flavorful, so just a little does the trick for adding lots of zing."

Chicken and Pepper Trio

Serving Size: 2 cups, Total Servings: 6

1 pound boneless, skinless chicken breast, cut into 1/2-inch strips

3/4 cup reduced-fat Italian dressing, divided

6 medium bell peppers (2 red, 2 green, 2 yellow), cut into thin strips

1 package (10 ounces) fresh spinach, washed and trimmed

1 Place the chicken in an 8-inch square baking dish and add 1/2 cup of the Italian dressing; mix well. Cover and marinate in the refrigerator for 1 hour.

2 Heat a large grill pan over high heat until hot. Place the chicken in the pan, discarding the marinade, and cook for 2 to 3 minutes per side, or until no pink remains. Remove the chicken from the pan; set aside. Add the peppers to the pan and cook for 4 to 5 minutes, or until crisp-tender, stirring occasionally.

3 Return the chicken to the pan and cook until heated through. Place the spinach in a large bowl and add the chicken mixture and the remaining 1/4 cup Italian dressing; toss well. Serve immediately.

Exchanges
2 Lean Meat
2 Vegetable

Calories 149
Calories from Fat . . . 27
Total Fat . . . . 3 g
Saturated Fat . . . . 1 g
Cholesterol . . . . 46 mg
Sodium . . . . 381 mg
Total Carbohydrate . . 12 g
Dietary Fiber . . . . 4 g
Sugars . . . . 4 g
Protein . . . . 19 g

"If you're looking for a tasty dish that's eye-catching, too, look no more, because what you see on the cover of this book is what you can have on your table in just minutes . . . honest!"

Chicken Under Wraps

Serving Size: 1 to 2 pieces, Total Servings: 5

1 whole chicken (3 pounds), skin removed

1 small onion, quartered

1/2 teaspoon rubbed sage

1/2 teaspoon paprika

2 garlic cloves, minced

1/4 teaspoon salt

1/4 teaspoon black pepper

4 to 5 large iceberg lettuce leaves, washed and patted dry

1 Preheat the oven to 350°F. Place the chicken breast side up in a 9" × 13" baking dish. Place the onion in the cavity of the chicken.

2 In a small bowl, combine the remaining ingredients except the lettuce; mix well. Rub the chicken evenly with the spice mixture, then lay the lettuce leaves over the top, curving them around to completely cover the chicken.

3 Bake the chicken for 80 to 90 minutes, or until no pink remains and the juices run clear. Discard the lettuce leaves and cut the chicken into serving-sized pieces.

Exchanges
4 Very Lean Meat
1/2 Fat

Calories 175
  Calories from Fat . . . 59
Total Fat . . . . 7 g
  Saturated Fat . . . . 2 g
Cholesterol . . . . 77 mg
Sodium . . . . 192 mg
Total Carbohydrate . . . 2 g
  Dietary Fiber . . . . 0 g
  Sugars . . . . 1 g
Protein . . . . 26 g

"By wrapping the skinless chicken in lettuce leaves, the bird stays really moist—with hardly any fat. Now that's something to crow about!"

Not-Fried "Fried" Chicken

Serving Size: 2 pieces, Total Servings: 5

Nonstick cooking spray

2 tablespoons all-purpose flour

1/2 teaspoon salt

1/4 teaspoon black pepper

3 egg whites

1-1/2 cups cornflake crumbs

1/2 teaspoon ground sage

1 chicken (3 to 3-1/2 pounds), cut into 10 pieces (cut each breast in half) and skin removed

1 Preheat the oven to 350°F. Coat a rimmed baking sheet with nonstick cooking spray.

2 In a shallow dish, combine the flour, salt, and pepper. In a medium bowl, lightly beat the egg whites. In a large bowl, combine the cornflake crumbs and sage.

3 Dip the chicken pieces in the flour mixture, then in the egg whites, then in the cornflake crumbs, coating completely with each. Place on the baking sheet. Lightly coat the top of the chicken with nonstick cooking spray and bake for 45 to 50 minutes, or until no pink remains and the juices run clear.

Exchanges
1-1/2 Starch
4 Very Lean Meat
1/2 Fat

Calories 299
Calories from Fat . . . 64
Total Fat . . . . 7 g
Saturated Fat . . . . 2 g
Cholesterol . . . . 84 mg
Sodium . . . . 627 mg
Total Carbohydrate . . 25 g
Dietary Fiber . . . . 1 g
Sugars . . . . 3 g
Protein . . . . 32 g

"Don't tell the ants, but we're going on a picnic! And it's simple when you let the oven do the advance work for you! Just bake this American oldie instead of making it in a hot, grease-filled fryer. Oh—you know what would be good with this? Green Bean and Tomato Toss (page 35). Have fun!"

Stovetop Shepherd's Pie

Serving Size: 1/8 recipe, Total Servings: 8

2 cups cubed cooked chicken (see Note)

1 package (16 ounces) frozen mixed vegetables, thawed and drained

1 can (10-3/4 ounces) 98% fat-free, reduced-sodium condensed cream of chicken soup

1/2 cup low-fat milk

1/4 teaspoon onion powder

1/4 teaspoon black pepper

3 cups hot mashed potatoes (instant or leftover), made with reduced-fat soft tub margarine and fat-free milk

1 In a large skillet, combine all the ingredients except the potatoes over high heat; mix well. Cook for 5 to 8 minutes, or until heated through, stirring frequently.

2 Remove from the heat and dollop with the potatoes. Serve immediately.

Note

Use leftover chicken or even turn to the deli case for thick-cut turkey breast— do what's easiest!

Exchanges

1-1/2 Starch
1 Lean Meat

Calories 185
  Calories from Fat . . . 38
Total Fat . . . . .4 g
  Saturated Fat . . . . . . 1.2 g
Cholesterol . . . . 36 mg
Sodium . . . . 311 mg
Total Carbohydrate . . 23 g
  Dietary Fiber . . . . .3 g
  Sugars . . . . .5 g
Protein . . . . 14 g

"This one's ideal for when the weather turns a little cooler, and it even comes with a bonus: you can use up almost any leftover veggies, chicken, or turkey that you have in the fridge to make it a truly stick-to-your-ribs meal."

Buffalo Chicken Strips

Serving Size: 3 strips, Total Servings: 5

1 tablespoon corn oil stick margarine

1-1/2 pounds boneless, skinless chicken breast, cut into 15 strips

1/4 cup hot cayenne pepper sauce

1 In a large skillet, melt the margarine over medium-high heat.

2 Add the chicken and hot pepper sauce and cook for up to 8 minutes, or until the chicken is no longer pink and the sauce thickens and coats the chicken. Serve immediately.

Finishing Touch

To capture that traditional Buffalo wing flavor, serve these with celery sticks and low-fat blue cheese dressing for dipping.

Exchanges
4 Very Lean Meat
1 Fat

Calories 176
   Calories from Fat . . . 50
Total Fat . . . . 6 g
   Saturated Fat . . . . . . 1.4 g
Cholesterol . . . . 79 mg
Sodium . . . . 164 mg
Total Carbohydrate . . . 0 g
   Dietary Fiber . . . . 0 g
   Sugars . . . . 0 g
Protein . . . . 29 g

Slim 'n' Trim Sausage Patties

Serving Size: 1 patty, Total Servings: 4

1 pound ground turkey breast

1 small onion, chopped

1/4 cup egg substitute

2 tablespoons dry bread crumbs

1 teaspoon ground thyme

1 teaspoon fennel seed

1/2 teaspoon garlic powder

1/4 teaspoon salt

1/2 teaspoon black pepper

1/4 teaspoon ground red pepper

1 Combine all the ingredients in a large bowl; mix well. Form the mixture into 4 equal-sized patties.

2 Coat a large nonstick skillet with nonstick cooking spray. Place the patties in the skillet and cook over medium heat for 3 to 4 minutes per side, or until no pink remains in the center.

Exchanges
1/2 Starch
3 Very Lean Meat

Calories 155
  Calories from Fat 9
Total Fat . . . . 1 g
  Saturated Fat . . . . 0 g
Cholesterol . . . . 70 mg
Sodium . . . . 259 mg
Total Carbohydrate . . . 5 g
  Dietary Fiber . . . . 0 g
  Sugars . . . . 2 g
Protein . . . . 30 g

"These turkey patties are packed with flavor all by themselves, though you'll probably want to serve them on whole-wheat buns with lettuce and tomato or maybe with lightly sautéed onions. Either way, since you're making them yourself (yes, you can do it!), they won't be full of fillers or fat."

Topless Sloppy Joes

Serving Size: 1 Sloppy Joe, Total Servings: 6

1 tablespoon canola oil

1 pound ground turkey breast

1 medium onion, chopped

1 rib celery, chopped

1/2 medium-sized green bell pepper, chopped

2 garlic cloves, minced

1 can (8 ounces) tomato sauce

1/4 cup Worcestershire sauce

3/4 cup water

1/8 teaspoon black pepper

3 hamburger buns, split

1 In a large skillet, heat the oil over medium-high heat and cook the turkey until browned, stirring to break up the meat.

2 Add the onion, celery, bell pepper, and garlic, and sauté for 5 minutes, stirring often.

3 Mix in the remaining ingredients except the buns and cook over medium heat for 10 minutes, or until thickened. Serve open-face–style over bun halves.

Exchanges

1 Starch
3 Very Lean Meat
1 Vegetable

Calories 201
Calories from Fat . . . 37
Total Fat . . . . 4 g
Saturated Fat . . . . 0 g
Cholesterol . . . . 47 mg
Sodium . . . . 522 mg
Total Carbohydrate . . 19 g
Dietary Fiber . . . . 2 g
Sugars . . . . 7 g
Protein . . . . 22 g

"Feeling daring? Go topless . . . with open-faced Sloppy Joes, I mean! It's a really tasty way to watch our carbs."

Cheddar–Turkey Burgers

1-1/2 pounds lean ground turkey breast

1/2 cup (2 ounces) reduced-fat shredded Cheddar cheese

1/2 teaspoon onion powder

1/2 teaspoon garlic powder

1/4 teaspoon salt

1 teaspoon black pepper

1 In a large bowl, combine all the ingredients; mix well. Form into 6 equal-sized patties.

2 Coat a large skillet with nonstick cooking spray and cook the patties over medium heat for 3 to 4 minutes per side, or until the juices run clear and no pink remains. Serve immediately.

Exchanges
3 Very Lean Meat

Calories 117
   Calories from Fat . . . 22
Total Fat . . . . 2 g
   Saturated Fat . . . . . . 1.3 g
Cholesterol . . . . 60 mg
Sodium . . . . 211 mg
Total Carbohydrate . . . 1 g
   Dietary Fiber . . . . 0 g
   Sugars . . . . 0 g
Protein . . . . 22 g

"Here's a lighter version of one of America's favorite meals. Whether they're cooked in a skillet or on the grill, these low-fat burgers will be gobbled up by the whole family. For another meal option, try making this into a meat loaf. Mmm mmm—two tasty recipes in one!"

Turkey Française

Serving Size: 1 cutlet, Total Servings: 6

1/2 cup all-purpose flour

1 tablespoon chopped fresh parsley

1/2 teaspoon salt

3/4 cup egg substitute

2 tablespoons olive oil

1-1/2 tablespoons corn oil stick margarine, divided

6 turkey cutlets (1-1/2 pounds total)

2/3 cup dry white wine

Juice of 1 lemon

1 In a shallow dish, combine the flour, parsley, and salt; mix well. Place the egg substitute in another shallow dish.

2 In a large skillet, heat the olive oil while melting 1 tablespoon margarine over medium heat. Dip the turkey in the flour mixture, then in the egg substitute, coating completely.

3 Sauté the turkey, in batches if necessary, for 2 to 3 minutes per side, or until golden. Add the remaining margarine, the wine, and lemon juice to the pan; mix well and return the cooked turkey to the skillet. Cook for 2 to 3 minutes, or until the sauce begins to thicken slightly. Serve the turkey topped with the sauce.

Exchanges
1/2 Starch
4 Very Lean Meat
1/2 Fat

Calories	249
Calories from Fat . . .	73
Total Fat	8 g
Saturated Fat	1.4 g
Cholesterol	74 mg
Sodium	330 mg
Total Carbohydrate . . .	9 g
Dietary Fiber	0 g
Sugars	1 g
Protein	31 g

Finishing Touch

This one's easy to fancy up by garnishing with lemon slices and a sprinkle of fresh chopped parsley just before serving. Take a look at Photo Insert B.

Roasted Veggies 'n' Turkey

Serving Size: 1/6 recipe, Total Servings: 6

3 tablespoons olive oil

2 tablespoons balsamic vinegar

1 teaspoon Italian seasoning

1/2 teaspoon salt

1/4 teaspoon black pepper

1-1/2 pounds boneless, skinless turkey cutlets, cut into thin strips

3 medium bell peppers (1 red, 1 yellow, and 1 green), cut into 2-inch pieces

2 medium-sized red onions, each cut into 6 wedges

2 large zucchini, cut into 1-inch pieces

1 Preheat the oven to 425°F. In a 9" × 13" baking dish, combine the oil, vinegar, Italian seasoning, salt, and black pepper. Add the turkey cutlets, bell peppers, onions, and zucchini; toss to coat completely.

2 Bake for 20 minutes. Turn the vegetables and turkey and baste with the pan juices. Roast for 10 to 15 more minutes, or until no pink remains in the turkey.

Exchanges

3 Vegetable
3 Very Lean Meat
1-1/2 Fat

Calories 241
   Calories from Fat . . . 70
Total Fat . . . . 8 g
   Saturated Fat . . . . . . 1.2 g
Cholesterol . . . . 74 mg
Sodium . . . . 255 mg
Total Carbohydrate . . 14 g
   Dietary Fiber . . . . 3 g
   Sugars . . . . 7 g
Protein . . . . 29 g

Citrus-Glazed Cornish Hens

Serving Size: 1 hen, Total Servings: 4

4 Cornish hens (1 pound each)

1 medium orange, quartered

1/2 teaspoon salt

1/4 teaspoon black pepper

1 package (4-serving size) sugar-free orange-flavored gelatin

1/4 cup honey

1/4 cup orange juice

1. Preheat the oven to 350°F. Coat a roasting pan with nonstick cooking spray. Place the Cornish hens in the pan; place an orange quarter into the cavity of each. Season with salt and pepper.

2. In a small bowl, combine the remaining ingredients and pour the mixture over the hens. Roast, uncovered, for 1-1/4 to 1-1/2 hours, or until no pink remains and the juices run clear, basting every 20 minutes.

3. Serve whole, or cut in half; drizzle with additional glaze from the pan.

Exchanges
1-1/2 Carbohydrate
6 Very Lean Meat

Calories	319
Calories from Fat	62
Total Fat	7 g
Saturated Fat	1.8 g
Cholesterol	190 mg
Sodium	462 mg
Total Carbohydrate	19 g
Dietary Fiber	0 g
Sugars	19 g
Protein	43 g

"These little birds are big on taste, thanks to the sugar-free gelatin and honey. Want to jazz 'em up a bit more? Sprinkle a little orange zest over them just before serving."

Nicole's Mediterranean Chicken

Serving Size: 1 cup, Total Servings: 4

2 tablespoons olive oil

1 pound boneless, skinless chicken breast, cut into 1-inch chunks

1 teaspoon dried basil

1 garlic clove, minced

1/2 small onion, diced

1/2 small green bell pepper, diced

1/2 small red bell pepper, diced

1/3 cup dry white wine

1 can (14-1/2 ounces) diced tomatoes

1/4 cup sliced pimiento-stuffed green olives

1/4 teaspoon black pepper

1 In a large skillet, heat the oil over medium heat. Add the chicken and basil to the skillet and brown the chicken, stirring frequently.

2 Add the remaining ingredients and cook, uncovered, for 20 minutes, or until the vegetables are tender and no pink remains in the chicken and the juices run clear.

Exchanges
3 Very Lean Meat
2 Vegetable
1-1/2 Fat

Calories 240
  Calories from Fat . . . 93
Total Fat . . . . 10 g
  Saturated Fat . . . . 2 g
Cholesterol . . . . 68 mg
Sodium . . . . 455 mg
Total Carbohydrate . . . 8 g
  Dietary Fiber . . . . 2 g
  Sugars . . . . 5 g
Protein . . . . 27 g

"My schedule keeps me on the road so much that when I get to stay home and cook a nice dinner for my family, this is the one I choose most often. The bit of wine that's in it makes it seem so elegant!"

Blackened Ostrich

Serving Size: 1 fillet, Total Servings: 2

1 teaspoon ground allspice

1 teaspoon dried thyme

1/4 teaspoon ground cinnamon

1/4 teaspoon garlic powder

1/4 teaspoon ground red pepper

1/8 teaspoon salt

2 ostrich fillets (6 ounces each)

1 teaspoon canola oil

1 In a small bowl, combine the allspice, thyme, cinnamon, garlic powder, ground red pepper, and salt; mix well. Place the fillets in the mixture and turn to coat completely.

2 Heat the oil in a medium skillet over medium-high heat. Cook the fillets for 4 to 5 minutes per side, or until desired doneness. Thinly slice each fillet, and serve.

Serving Tip

This becomes even more special when served with a corn salsa made by combining a small can of drained whole kernel corn, 2 chopped scallions, a seeded and chopped plum tomato, 1-1/2 teaspoons apple cider vinegar, 1 tablespoon chopped cilantro, and 1 teaspoon ground cumin. I like to make the salsa ahead of time and serve it chilled with the warm ostrich.

Exchanges

5 Very Lean Meat
1/2 Fat

Calories 201
  Calories from Fat . . . 54
Total Fat . . . . 6 g
  Saturated Fat . . . . 0 g
Cholesterol . . . . 122 mg
Sodium . . . . 239 mg
Total Carbohydrate . . . 0 g
  Dietary Fiber . . . . 0 g
  Sugars . . . . 0 g
Protein . . . . 34 g

"Whoa! Ostrich?! Trust me on this one! Ostrich is extremely low in fat, and, even though it's considered poultry, its taste is similar to beef. It's in most of our supermarkets now, so give it a try. I promise, one bite and you'll be a believer!"

Mouthwatering Meats

Steak Provençal

Serving Size: 1/6 recipe, Total Servings: 6

1 tablespoon canola oil

1 pound boneless beef top sirloin steak, cut into 1-inch chunks

1 large onion, chopped

3 garlic cloves, minced

1/2 teaspoon black pepper

3 yellow squash, cut into 1-inch chunks

1 can (15 ounces) Great Northern beans, rinsed and drained

1 can (14-1/2 ounces) diced tomatoes

2 tablespoons chopped fresh basil

2 cups loosely-packed fresh spinach leaves, trimmed

1 tablespoon grated Parmesan cheese

1 In a soup pot, heat the oil over high heat. Add the steak, onion, garlic, and pepper. Sauté for 6 to 8 minutes, or until the steak and onions are browned, stirring frequently.

2 Add the yellow squash, reduce the heat to medium, and cook for 3 to 4 minutes, or until the squash is tender. Add the beans, tomatoes, and basil; mix well. Cook for 3 to 4 more minutes, or until heated through.

3 Just before serving, stir in the spinach and cook for 2 to 3 minutes, or until the spinach wilts. Sprinkle with the Parmesan cheese and serve.

Exchanges
1 Starch
2 Lean Meat
2 Vegetable

Calories 233
  Calories from Fat . . . 60
Total Fat . . . . 7 g
  Saturated Fat . . . . 1 g
Cholesterol . . . . 44 mg
Sodium . . . . 301 mg
Total Carbohydrate . . 23 g
  Dietary Fiber . . . . 6 g
  Sugars . . . . 8 g
Protein . . . . 22 g

"Check out this colorful Continental treat in Photo Insert C."

Inside-Out Steak

3 tablespoons olive oil

2 tablespoons red wine vinegar

1 scallion, thinly sliced

2 garlic cloves, minced

1/2 teaspoon salt

1 teaspoon pepper

1 2-pound beef flank steak, about 1 inch thick

1 In a large resealable plastic storage bag, combine all the ingredients except the steak; mix well. Score the steak on both sides by making shallow diagonal cuts 1-1/2 inches apart. Place the steak in the storage bag, seal, and marinate in the refrigerator for at least 4 hours, or overnight, turning the bag over occasionally.

2 Heat a large grill pan over high heat until hot. Remove the steak from the marinade and place in the pan; discard the marinade. Cook the steak for 4 to 5 minutes per side for medium-rare, or until desired doneness beyond that.

3 Thinly slice the steak across the grain and serve.

Exchanges
3 Lean Meat

Calories	172
Calories from Fat	76
Total Fat	8 g
Saturated Fat	2.8 g
Cholesterol	39 mg
Sodium	119 mg
Total Carbohydrate	0 g
Dietary Fiber	0 g
Sugars	0 g
Protein	22 g

Finishing Touch

Why not give this more color by sprinkling with additional scallion slices before serving?

Singapore Stir-Fry

1 tablespoon vegetable oil

1 1-1/2-pound beef flank steak, 1 inch thick, cut into thin strips

1/2 cup sweet-and-sour sauce

3 tablespoons light soy sauce

2 tablespoons minced garlic

1 tablespoon ground ginger

1/2 teaspoon hot pepper sauce

1/2 teaspoon black pepper

1 package (16 ounces) frozen stir-fry vegetable mix, thawed and drained

1. In a large skillet, heat the oil over medium heat. Add the steak strips and brown for 5 to 6 minutes per side.

2. Meanwhile, in a small bowl, combine the sweet-and-sour sauce, soy sauce, garlic, ginger, hot pepper sauce, and black pepper. Add to the steak along with the vegetables.

3. Reduce the heat to low and simmer for 3 to 5 minutes, stirring until completely mixed and heated through.

Good for You!

Although the Internet will never replace your doctor, it does provide plenty of sites where you can get answers to commonly asked questions about diabetes. In case you don't already have it, the web address of the American Diabetes Association is http://www.diabetes.org. Check it out!

Exchanges
1/2 Carbohydrate
1 Vegetable
3 Lean Meat

Calories 233
  Calories from Fat . . . 74
Total Fat . . . . 8 g
  Saturated Fat . . . . . . 2.6 g
Cholesterol . . . . 39 mg
Sodium . . . . 483 mg
Total Carbohydrate . . 13 g
  Dietary Fiber . . . . 2 g
  Sugars . . . . 8 g
Protein . . . . 24 g

Crispy-Crusted Steak

Serving Size: 1 steak, Total Servings: 4

1/2 cup cornflake crumbs

1 tablespoon dried flaked minced onion

2 tablespoons olive oil

2 teaspoons spicy brown mustard

4 thinly sliced beef top round steaks (1 pound total)

1 Place the broiler rack 8 to 10 inches from the heat source and preheat the broiler. Place the cornflake crumbs and minced onion in a shallow dish; mix well.

2 In another shallow dish, combine the oil and the mustard. Dip the steaks into the oil mixture, then into the cornflake mixture, lightly coating with each.

3 Place the steaks on a rimmed baking sheet and broil for 3 to 4 minutes per side, or until cooked through.

Exchanges

1/2 Starch
3 Lean Meat

Calories	235
Calories from Fat	106
Total Fat	12 g
Saturated Fat	2.6 g
Cholesterol	58 mg
Sodium	208 mg
Total Carbohydrate	11 g
Dietary Fiber	1 g
Sugars	2 g
Protein	20 g

"What's the difference between a meal plan for people with diabetes and a meal plan for everyone else? Choosing the healthiest ingredients, balancing carbs and calories, and not eating 'til you're stuffed! Who wouldn't benefit from following a low-fat, high-fiber, tasty meal plan?!"

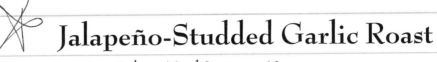

Jalapeño-Studded Garlic Roast

Serving Size: 3 to 4 slices, Total Servings: 10

1 3-pound beef eye of the round roast

1 jalapeño pepper, cut into 20 pieces (see below)

20 garlic cloves

6 scallions

1 teaspoon browning and seasoning sauce

1 teaspoon salt

1/4 teaspoon ground red pepper

1 Preheat the oven to 400°F. Coat a roasting pan with nonstick cooking spray. With a sharp knife, carefully pierce the surface of the roast evenly 20 times, making each slit about 1-1/2 inches deep. Stuff a piece of jalapeño pepper and a clove of garlic in each slit.

2 Place the scallions in the roasting pan and place the roast over the scallions. Brush the roast with the browning and seasoning sauce. Season with the salt and ground red pepper and roast for 45 to 60 minutes, or until the roast reaches the desired doneness.

3 Remove the roast to a cutting board. Slice thinly and spoon pan juices over each serving.

Exchanges
4 Very Lean Meat
1/2 Fat

Calories 163
 Calories from Fat . . . 39
Total Fat . . . . 4 g
 Saturated Fat . . . . 2 g
Cholesterol . . . . 62 mg
Sodium . . . . 293 mg
Total Carbohydrate . . . 3 g
 Dietary Fiber . . . . 1 g
 Sugars . . . . 2 g
Protein . . . . 26 g

"When handling hot peppers, I've found that if I lightly coat my hands with vegetable oil, I don't feel the sting of the juices and seeds. It's sort of like wearing gloves. But take care—the oil on your hands will also make kitchen utensils (including knives!) very slippery! And even if you've coated your hands, don't forget to keep them away from your eyes and mouth!"

Caramelized Cola Roast

Serving Size: 2 to 3 slices, Total Servings: 9

1 3-pound very lean beef bottom round roast

1/2 teaspoon salt

1/2 teaspoon pepper

1/2 teaspoon garlic powder

1 cup diet cola

1/2 cup chili sauce

1 tablespoon Worcestershire sauce

1 Preheat the oven to 325°F. Coat a roasting pan with nonstick cooking spray and place the roast in the pan. Season with the salt, pepper, and garlic powder.

2 In a small bowl, combine the remaining ingredients and pour over the roast. Cover with aluminum foil and roast for 2-1/2 to 3 hours, or until tender.

3 Slice, and serve topped with the sauce from the pan.

Exchanges
4 Lean Meat

Calories 234
Calories from Fat . . . 72
Total Fat . . . . 8 g
Saturated Fat . . . . . . 2.8 g
Cholesterol . . . . 108 mg
Sodium . . . . 376 mg
Total Carbohydrate . . . 4 g
Dietary Fiber . . . . 0 g
Sugars . . . . 2 g
Protein . . . . 35 g

"Can you believe that a regular cola has NINE teaspoons of sugar and practically three times as many grams of carbohydrates as a diet cola?! The choice is easy, and since they taste so similar, nobody will be able to tell the difference in this recipe."

Tarragon Pot Roast

Serving Size: 2 to 3 slices, Total Servings: 9

1 3-pound very lean beef bottom round roast

1 medium onion, chopped

2 carrots, sliced

1/2 cup dry red wine

1/2 cup water

1 tablespoon minced garlic

1 tablespoon dried tarragon

1/4 teaspoon black pepper

1 Preheat the oven to 325°F. Coat a roasting pan with nonstick cooking spray and place the roast in the pan.

2 In a medium bowl, combine the remaining ingredients and pour over the roast. Bake for 1-1/2 to 2 hours, or until the meat is fork-tender.

3 Slice, and serve topped with the sauce from the pan.

Exchanges
4 Lean Meat

Calories 235
  Calories from Fat . . . 72
Total Fat . . . . 8 g
  Saturated Fat . . . . . . 2.8 g
Cholesterol . . . . 108 mg
Sodium . . . . 55 mg
Total Carbohydrate . . . 4 g
  Dietary Fiber . . . . 1 g
  Sugars . . . . 1 g
Protein . . . . 35 g

New World Sauerbraten

3 tablespoons vegetable oil

2 tablespoons apple cider vinegar

1 can (12 ounces) diet ginger ale

1/3 cup lemon juice

3/4 teaspoon garlic powder

1/8 teaspoon ground cloves

1/2 teaspoon salt

1/4 teaspoon pepper

1 small onion, chopped

1 2-pound beef top round (1-1/2 inches thick)

1 tablespoon cornstarch

1 In a large resealable plastic storage bag, combine all the ingredients except the beef and cornstarch. Add the beef, seal, and refrigerate for at least 8 hours or overnight, turning occasionally.

2 Remove the beef from the marinade and place in a large skillet. Add the cornstarch to the marinade; mix well and set aside. Brown the beef over medium-high heat for 5 minutes per side. Reduce the heat to medium-low, add the marinade mixture, cover, and cook for 30 minutes.

3 Uncover and cook for another 30 to 40 minutes, or until desired doneness. Thinly slice the meat across the grain and serve with the pan juices.

Exchanges
3 Lean Meat
1/2 Fat

Calories 191
  Calories from Fat . . . 80
Total Fat . . . . 9 g
  Saturated Fat . . . . 1 g
Cholesterol . . . . 58 mg
Sodium . . . . 180 mg
Total Carbohydrate . . . 3 g
  Dietary Fiber . . . . 0 g
  Sugars . . . . 1 g
Protein . . . . 24 g

"The longer this beef is marinated, the more flavor it will retain while cooking. And if there's any left over, enjoy it on open-faced sandwiches tomorrow for lunch!"

Weekend Beef Stew

Serving Size: 1-1/2 cups, Total Servings: 6

3 tablespoons all-purpose flour

1 pound beef flank steak, cut into 1/2-inch chunks

3 tablespoons canola oil

2 cups water

1 cup decaffeinated black coffee

1 teaspoon dried thyme

1 teaspoon salt

1 teaspoon black pepper

6 medium potatoes, peeled and quartered

6 carrots, cut into large chunks

3 medium onions, quartered

1 teaspoon browning and seasoning sauce

1 Place the flour in a shallow dish; add the beef chunks and coat completely with the flour. In a soup pot, heat the oil over medium-high heat; add the beef and brown on all sides for 8 to 10 minutes.

2 Add the water, coffee, thyme, salt, and pepper to the beef; mix well and bring to a boil. Reduce the heat to low, cover, and simmer for 1 hour.

3 Add the remaining ingredients, increase the heat to high and return to a boil. Reduce the heat to low and simmer for 50 to 60 minutes, or until the beef and vegetables are tender, stirring occasionally.

Exchanges
2 Starch
3 Vegetable
1 Lean Meat
1-1/2 Fat

Calories 357
 Calories from Fat . . 112
Total Fat . . . . 12 g
 Saturated Fat . . . . . . 2.8 g
Cholesterol . . . . 35 mg
Sodium . . . . 505 mg
Total Carbohydrate . . 43 g
 Dietary Fiber . . . . 6 g
 Sugars . . . . 9 g
Protein . . . . 18 g

"Why not make this hearty stew on the weekend and freeze it in single-serve containers for quick lunches or dinners in the weeks to come?"

Guilt-Free Beef Stroganoff

Serving Size: 1/8 recipe, Total Servings: 8

1 1-pound boneless beef top sirloin steak, well trimmed and thinly sliced across the grain

1 small onion, chopped

1 pound fresh sliced mushrooms

1 can (10-3/4 ounces) condensed reduced-fat cream of mushroom soup

1 cup dry white wine

1/4 teaspoon black pepper

1 pound uncooked no-yolk egg noodles

1/2 cup reduced-fat sour cream

2 tablespoons chopped fresh parsley

1 Coat a nonstick skillet with nonstick cooking spray. Add the steak and onion and brown over medium-high heat for 5 to 7 minutes, or until no pink remains in the steak and the onions are tender, stirring occasionally.

2 Add the mushrooms and cook for 3 minutes, or until tender. Reduce the heat to medium-low and stir in the soup, wine, and pepper; simmer for 25 minutes, or until the steak is tender.

3 Prepare the noodles according to the package directions, omitting the salt; drain, then set aside and cover to keep warm.

4 Add the sour cream and parsley to the steak mixture, and cook for 1 minute, or until heated through; do not boil. Serve over the warm noodles.

Exchanges
3 Starch
2 Very Lean Meat
1 Vegetable

Calories 342
   Calories from Fat . . . 47
Total Fat . . . . 5 g
   Saturated Fat . . . . 2 g
Cholesterol . . . . 38 mg
Sodium . . . . 212 mg
Total Carbohydrate . . 48 g
   Dietary Fiber . . . . 4 g
   Sugars . . . . 6 g
Protein . . . . 22 g

"Didn't think you could have such a rich and creamy main dish? Well, think again! Using ingredients with reduced fat and no-yolk noodles lets us indulge in oh-so-tasty dinners without cheating on our meal plans."

Homestyle Meat Loaf

Serving Size: 1 slice, Total Servings: 10

2 pounds 95% lean ground beef

1 can (8-1/4 ounces) julienne carrots, drained

1 can (13-1/2 ounces) mushroom stems and pieces, drained

1/2 cup cornflake crumbs — *Stuffing mix*

1 tablespoon dried minced onion

1/2 cup egg substitute

1/2 teaspoon black pepper

3 tablespoons ketchup

1. Preheat the oven to 350°F. Coat a 5" × 9" loaf pan with nonstick cooking spray.

2. In a large bowl, combine the ground beef, carrots, mushrooms, cornflake crumbs, minced onion, egg substitute, and pepper; mix well. Place in the loaf pan and spread the ketchup evenly over the top.

3. Bake for 1-1/2 hours, or until no pink remains. Allow to sit for 5 minutes. Pour off excess liquid, if any, then slice and serve.

Exchanges
1/2 Carbohydrate
2 Lean Meat

Calories 163
  Calories from Fat . . . 44
Total Fat . . . . 5 g
  Saturated Fat . . . . . . 2.1 g
Cholesterol . . . . 55 mg
Sodium . . . . 281 mg
Total Carbohydrate . . . 8 g
  Dietary Fiber . . . . 1 g
  Sugars . . . . 2 g
Protein . . . . 21 g

"Got a craving for comfort food? It's meat loaf to the rescue! Not only is it great for dinner, but some (like me!) say it's even better 'the day after' as the filling in a cold meat loaf sandwich."

Chunky Sloppy Joes

Serving Size: 1 sandwich, Total Servings: 8

1 pound lean ground beef

1 small zucchini, chopped

1 small onion, chopped

1 small tomato, chopped

2 cups light spaghetti sauce

8 hamburger buns, split

1 In a large skillet, brown the ground beef, zucchini, and onion over medium-high heat for 10 to 12 minutes, or until the beef is no longer pink and the zucchini is tender.

2 Reduce the heat to medium-low and stir in the tomato and the spaghetti sauce. Cook for 4 to 5 minutes, or until heated through.

3 Spoon over the bottom halves of the buns, cover with the bun tops, and serve immediately.

Exchanges
2 Starch
1 Medium-Fat Meat
1/2 Fat

Calories 267
  Calories from Fat . . . 87
Total Fat . . . . 10 g
  Saturated Fat . . . . 3 g
Cholesterol . . . . 36 mg
Sodium . . . . 586 mg
Total Carbohydrate . . 29 g
  Dietary Fiber . . . . 3 g
  Sugars . . . . 8 g
Protein . . . . 15 g

"Adding veggies to our protein is a great way to fill out and stretch our meals without going over our limits."

Lemon Pork Tenderloin

Serving Size: 4 to 6 slices, Total Servings: 8

1/4 cup plus 1 tablespoon olive oil, divided

Juice of 2 lemons (1/4 cup)

4 garlic cloves, halved

2 well-trimmed pork tenderloins (about 2 pounds total)

2 tablespoons light brown sugar

1/2 teaspoon salt

1 In a large resealable plastic storage bag or a shallow dish, combine 1/4 cup olive oil, the lemon juice, and garlic; add the tenderloins. Seal the bag or cover the dish and refrigerate for 30 minutes, turning the tenderloins after 15 minutes.

2 Heat the remaining 1 tablespoon olive oil in a large skillet over medium-high heat. Place the tenderloins in the skillet, reserving the marinade. Cook for 10 to 12 minutes, until cooked to medium, or to desired doneness beyond that, turning to brown on all sides.

3 Remove to a cutting board and cover to keep warm. Place the reserved marinade, the brown sugar, and salt in the skillet and bring to a boil. Reduce the heat to low and simmer for 5 minutes.

4 Slice the pork, and serve topped with the sauce.

Exchanges
3 Lean Meat
1 Fat

Calories 228
  Calories from Fat . . 112
Total Fat . . . . 12 g
  Saturated Fat . . . . . . 2.5 g
Cholesterol . . . . 66 mg
Sodium . . . . 195 mg
Total Carbohydrate . . . 4 g
  Dietary Fiber . . . . 0 g
  Sugars . . . . 4 g
Protein . . . . 24 g

Skillet Pork Chops

Serving Size: 1 chop, Total Servings: 4

4 pork loin chops (8 ounces each), well trimmed

1/4 teaspoon ground cinnamon

1/4 teaspoon salt

1/4 teaspoon pepper

2 tablespoons canola oil

2 medium onions, cut into 6 wedges each

3 medium carrots, cut into 1-inch chunks

1 Season both sides of the pork chops with the cinnamon, salt, and pepper.

2 In a large skillet, heat the oil over medium-high heat. Brown the pork chops for 4 to 5 minutes per side.

3 Add the onions and carrots to the skillet. Reduce the heat to low, cover, and cook for 25 to 30 minutes, or until the vegetables are tender and the pork chops are cooked through. Serve the vegetables with the pork chops.

Exchanges
3 Vegetable
4 Lean Meat
1 Fat

Calories 340
  Calories from Fat . . 146
Total Fat . . . . 16 g
  Saturated Fat . . . . . . 3.9 g
Cholesterol . . . . 94 mg
Sodium . . . . 257 mg
Total Carbohydrate . . 13 g
  Dietary Fiber . . . . 3 g
  Sugars . . . . 6 g
Protein . . . . 34 g

"This is great served with Garlic Mashed Potatoes (see page 152)."

Herb-Roasted Pork Chops

Serving Size: 1 chop, Total Servings: 4

3 tablespoons fresh lemon juice

3 scallions, thinly sliced

3 garlic cloves, minced

1-1/2 teaspoons dried rosemary, crushed

1/4 teaspoon black pepper

4 pork chops (6 ounces each), well trimmed

Nonstick cooking spray

1. Preheat the oven to 400°F. Coat an 8-inch square baking dish with nonstick cooking spray.

2. In a shallow dish, combine the lemon juice, scallions, garlic, rosemary, and pepper. Dip each pork chop into the lemon mixture, coating completely, then place in the baking dish.

3. Lightly coat the chops with nonstick cooking spray. Bake for 15 to 20 minutes, or until desired doneness.

Exchanges
3 Lean Meat

Calories	182
Calories from Fat	65
Total Fat	7 g
Saturated Fat	2.7 g
Cholesterol	71 mg
Sodium	57 mg
Total Carbohydrate	3 g
Dietary Fiber	1 g
Sugars	1 g
Protein	25 g

"Do you have a friend (or friends) with diabetes? Do what I do and challenge him/her/them to see who can have the best A1C level every 3 months. The extra motivation takes us all a long way . . . especially 'cause the one with the lowest level gets taken out for a fancy dinner!"

Jammin' Pork Tenderloin

Serving Size: 4 to 5 slices, Total Servings: 8

1/4 cup honey

1/3 cup lime juice

1 teaspoon grated lime peel

2 garlic cloves, minced

2 tablespoons yellow mustard

1/2 teaspoon salt

1/2 teaspoon pepper

2 pork tenderloins (2 pounds total), well trimmed

1 In a large resealable plastic storage bag, combine all the ingredients except the tenderloins; mix well. Add the tenderloins, seal, and marinate in the refrigerator for at least 4 hours, or overnight, turning the bag occasionally.

2 Preheat the broiler. Place the pork on a broiler pan or rimmed baking sheet; discard the marinade. Broil for 7 to 9 minutes per side, or until desired doneness.

3 Slice the tenderloins across the grain and serve.

Good for You!

Pork tenderloin is one of the leanest cuts available at the supermarket meat department. If trimmed, a single portion has only 1 gram of saturated fat. That's why it's such a healthy choice!

Exchanges

1/2 Carbohydrate
3 Very Lean Meat
1/2 Fat

Calories 154
   Calories from Fat . . . 38
Total Fat . . . . 4 g
   Saturated Fat . . . . 1 g
Cholesterol . . . . 65 mg
Sodium . . . . 144 mg
Total Carbohydrate . . . 5 g
   Dietary Fiber . . . . 0 g
   Sugars . . . . 5 g
Protein . . . . 24 g

Tomato–Basil Veal

Serving Size: 1 cutlet, Total Servings: 4

- **1/4** cup whole-wheat flour
- **1/4** teaspoon salt
- **1/4** teaspoon pepper
- **2** tablespoons canola oil
- **4** veal cutlets (1 pound total)
- **1/4** cup sun-dried tomatoes, reconstituted and slivered
- **3** tablespoons chopped fresh basil, divided

1 In a shallow dish, combine the whole-wheat flour, salt, and pepper; mix well. Place the veal in the flour mixture and turn to coat completely.

2 Heat the oil in a large skillet over medium-high heat. Add the veal, sun-dried tomatoes, and 2 tablespoons of the basil. Sauté the veal for 2 to 3 minutes per side, or until browned and cooked through.

3 Sprinkle with the remaining basil and serve.

Exchanges
1/2 Starch
3 Lean Meat
1/2 Fat

Calories 231	
Calories from Fat . . . 95	
Total Fat . . . . 11 g	
Saturated Fat . . . . . . 1.7 g	
Cholesterol . . . . 90 mg	
Sodium . . . . 191 mg	
Total Carbohydrate . . . 7 g	
Dietary Fiber . . . . 1 g	
Sugars . . . . 1 g	
Protein . . . . 26 g	

"Like many of today's working folks, Nicole has a nonstop schedule requiring healthy meals that are ready in a snap. I promised her that she can literally get this from the stovetop to the tabletop in less than 20 minutes. She found out I was right . . . and so can you!"

Sensational Seafood

Pistachio-Crusted Mahimahi

Serving Size: 1 fillet, Total Servings: 6

6 fresh mahimahi fillets
(5 ounces each)

Juice of 1 lemon

1/2 teaspoon ground nutmeg

1/4 teaspoon black pepper

Salt to taste

1/2 cup coarsely chopped pistachio
nuts

2 tablespoons butter, melted

1 Preheat the oven to 350°F. Place
the mahimahi fillets on a rimmed
baking sheet. Season with the lemon
juice, nutmeg, pepper, and salt if
desired. Top with the pistachio nuts
and drizzle with the melted butter.

2 Bake for 20 to 22 minutes, or
until the fish flakes easily with a
fork. Serve immediately.

Good for You!

*Different nuts have different
nutritional values, and pistachios are among the
lowest in saturated fat and cholesterol, so when
deciding on a type for snacking, read the package
labels to make sure you keep within your
own dietary guidelines.*

Exchanges
4 Lean Meat

Calories 222
Calories from Fat . . . 94
Total Fat . . . . 10 g
Saturated Fat . . . . 3 g
Cholesterol . . . . 115 mg
Sodium . . . . 167 mg
Total Carbohydrate . . . 3 g
Dietary Fiber . . . . 1 g
Sugars . . . . 1 g
Protein . . . . 28 g

Crusted Salmon

Serving Size: 1 salmon steak, Total Servings: 4

4 salmon steaks (5 ounces each)

1/3 cup fat-free mayonnaise

1 tablespoon fresh lemon juice

1 garlic clove, minced

1 teaspoon dried dillweed

1/4 teaspoon salt

1/4 teaspoon pepper

1 Preheat the broiler. Coat a broiler pan or rimmed baking sheet with nonstick cooking spray. Place the salmon steaks on the pan.

2 In a small bowl, combine all the remaining ingredients; mix well. Spread evenly over the top of the salmon steaks, then broil for 10 to 12 minutes, or until the fish flakes easily with a fork. Serve immediately.

Exchanges
4 Lean Meat
1/2 Fat

Calories 256
  Calories from Fat . . 109
Total Fat . . . . 12 g
  Saturated Fat . . . . . . 2.1 g
Cholesterol . . . . 96 mg
Sodium . . . . 380 mg
Total Carbohydrate . . . 4 g
  Dietary Fiber . . . . 0 g
  Sugars . . . . 1 g
Protein . . . . 30 g

"Many people are reluctant to make fish at home because they think it's a complicated process. Well, this quick recipe has just two steps. How easy is that? While broiling, the mayonnaise mixture puffs up and seals in the juices to keep the fish extra moist."

Cajun Halibut

Serving Size: 1 halibut steak, Total Servings: 4

1/4 teaspoon salt

1 teaspoon black pepper

1/4 teaspoon ground red pepper

1/4 teaspoon paprika

1/4 teaspoon garlic powder

4 halibut steaks (4 ounces each)

1 In a small bowl, combine the salt, black and ground red peppers, paprika, and garlic powder; mix well. Rub evenly over both sides of the fish.

2 Preheat a large nonstick skillet over medium-high heat. When hot, remove from the heat and, away from the cooking surface, coat with nonstick cooking spray.

3 Return the skillet to the heat, add the fish, and cook for 3 to 4 minutes per side, or until the fish is cooked through and flakes easily with a fork. Serve immediately.

Exchanges
4 Very Lean Meat

Calories 126
Calories from Fat . . . 23
Total Fat . . . . 3 g
Saturated Fat . . . . 0 g
Cholesterol . . . . 37 mg
Sodium . . . . 208 mg
Total Carbohydrate . . . 0 g
Dietary Fiber . . . . 0 g
Sugars . . . . 0 g
Protein . . . . 24 g

Note

If you want to enjoy this in a less spicy version, try cutting the amount of black and ground red peppers by half.

Mussels Pomodoro

Serving Size: 1/8 recipe, Total Servings: 8

1 pound spaghetti

2 pounds mussels, cleaned (see Note)

1 can (14-1/2 ounces) stewed tomatoes

1/4 cup dry white wine

2 garlic cloves, minced

1/2 teaspoon dried oregano

1/4 teaspoon black pepper

1 Cook the spaghetti according to the package directions, omitting the salt; drain.

2 Meanwhile, in a soup pot, combine the remaining ingredients over high heat; bring to a boil. Reduce the heat to low, cover, and cook for 2 to 3 minutes, or until the mussels open. **Discard any unopened mussels.**

3 Serve the spaghetti in bowls topped with the mussels and sauce.

Note

If you buy mussels that aren't cleaned and ready for cooking, here's what to do: Wash them under cold, running water, and scrub away any grit or barnacles with a stiff food scrub brush. Remove the black beard from each mussel by cutting or pulling it off.

Exchanges

3 Starch
1 Very Lean Meat

Calories 285
  Calories from Fat . . . 23
Total Fat . . . . 3 g
  Saturated Fat . . . . 0 g
Cholesterol . . . . 18 mg
Sodium . . . . 254 mg
Total Carbohydrate . . 49 g
  Dietary Fiber . . . . 2 g
  Sugars . . . . 6 g
Protein . . . . 15 g

Salmon Florentine

Serving Size: 1 salmon fillet, Total Servings: 4

1 tablespoon olive oil

4 garlic cloves, minced

1/4 teaspoon black pepper

1 package (10 ounces) fresh spinach, washed and trimmed

4 salmon fillets (5 ounces each)

Juice of 1/2 lemon

1/4 teaspoon dried basil

1 In a soup pot, heat the oil over medium heat. Add the garlic and pepper and sauté for 1 minute, until the garlic is golden.

2 Add the spinach and toss to coat. Place the salmon fillets over the spinach and sprinkle with the lemon juice and basil.

3 Reduce the heat to medium-low, cover, and cook for 10 to 12 minutes, or until the spinach is wilted and the salmon flakes easily with a fork. Serve fillets topped with spinach.

Did You Know . . .

that even though salmon is considered a fatty fish, it is an excellent source of omega-3 fatty acids, which promote cardiovascular health? Salmon is also packed with protein and virtually devoid of carbohydrates. Now that's what I call a ship-shape food!

Exchanges
4 Lean Meat
1 Fat

Calories 291
  Calories from Fat . . 142
Total Fat . . . . 16 g
  Saturated Fat . . . . . . 2.6 g
Cholesterol . . . . 96 mg
Sodium . . . . 130 mg
Total Carbohydrate . . . 4 g
  Dietary Fiber . . . . 2 g
  Sugars . . . . 0 g
Protein . . . . 32 g

Baked Fish "Fry"

2 egg whites, beaten

1/2 teaspoon dried dillweed

1/2 teaspoon black pepper

1 cup cornflake crumbs

2 pounds fresh or frozen haddock fillets, thawed if frozen, cut into 8 pieces

Nonstick cooking spray

1 Preheat the oven to 400°F. Coat a baking sheet with nonstick cooking spray.

2 In a shallow bowl, combine the egg whites, dillweed, and pepper. Place the cornflake crumbs in another shallow bowl. Dip the fish in the egg mixture, then in the cornflake crumbs, coating completely. Place the fish on the baking sheet.

3 Coat the fish with nonstick cooking spray and bake for 18 to 20 minutes, or until it flakes easily with a fork.

Exchanges
1/2 Starch
3 Very Lean Meat

Calories 144
   Calories from Fat 8
Total Fat . . . . 1 g
   Saturated Fat . . . . 0 g
Cholesterol . . . . 65 mg
Sodium . . . . 208 mg
Total Carbohydrate . . 10 g
   Dietary Fiber . . . . 0 g
   Sugars . . . . 1 g
Protein . . . . 23 g

"You're gonna be ahead of the game by baking this fish in the oven instead of deep-frying it. Everybody benefits by having less fat in his or her diet, right? Absolutely right!"

Garlic Shrimp Linguine

Serving Size: 1/8 recipe, Total Servings: 8

1 pound linguine

2 tablespoons olive oil

2 tablespoons corn oil stick margarine

2 medium zucchini, quartered lengthwise and sliced

12 garlic cloves, minced

1/2 teaspoon salt

1/2 teaspoon pepper

1 pound medium-sized shrimp (20 to 30 per pound), peeled and deveined with tails left on

1/4 cup dry white wine

3 tablespoons chopped fresh parsley

2 tablespoons fresh lemon juice

1 Cook the linguine according to the package directions, omitting the salt; drain.

2 Meanwhile, in a large skillet, heat the oil and margarine over medium heat. Add the zucchini, garlic, salt, and pepper, and sauté for 3 to 4 minutes, until the zucchini starts to soften. Add the shrimp, wine, and parsley and sauté for 2 to 3 minutes, until the shrimp turn pink.

3 Pour the shrimp mixture over the linguine, add the lemon juice, and toss. Serve immediately.

Exchanges

3 Starch
1 Very Lean Meat
1 Fat

Calories	317
Calories from Fat	69
Total Fat	8 g
Saturated Fat	1.2 g
Cholesterol	65 mg
Sodium	258 mg
Total Carbohydrate	46 g
Dietary Fiber	3 g
Sugars	3 g
Protein	15 g

"If you love garlic (and who doesn't!), you'll love this dish that's chock-full of it. Surprisingly, the garlic doesn't overpower any of the other flavors."

Frogmore Stew

Serving Size: 1/6 recipe, Total Servings: 6

8 cups water

1 tablespoon salt-free seafood seasoning

1/4 teaspoon ground red pepper

3/4 pound turkey kielbasa sausage, cut into 2-inch pieces

3 medium potatoes, cut in half

3 medium onions, cut in half

2 large ears corn, husked and cut into 3-inch pieces

1 pound medium (20 to 30 per pound) shrimp, unpeeled

1 In a soup pot, combine the water, seafood seasoning, and ground red pepper and bring to a boil over high heat.

2 Add the sausage, potatoes, onions, and corn, and cook for 15 to 20 minutes, or until the potatoes are fork-tender. Add the shrimp and cook for 2 to 3 minutes, or until the shrimp are pink and cooked through.

3 Strain the stew and serve immediately, along with bowls of broth for dunking.

Did You Know . . .

that this stew with the funny name is the clambake of the South? It hails from the Carolinas where, the story goes, it was created when a National Guardsman cleaned out his fridge and threw leftover shrimp, sausage, corn, and a handful of spices into a big pot and boiled it all. The traditional way to experience it is to cover the table with clean newspaper, then boil up the stew, drain it, and dump it out onto the newspaper where everybody can pick up what they want and go to it. Just make sure you save the broth for dunking!

Exchanges
2 Starch
1 Vegetable
2 Lean Meat

Calories 274
  Calories from Fat . . . 54
Total Fat . . . . 6 g
  Saturated Fat . . . . . . 2.2 g
Cholesterol . . . . 119 mg
Sodium . . . . 717 mg
Total Carbohydrate . . 36 g
  Dietary Fiber . . . . 4 g
  Sugars . . . . 8 g
Protein . . . . 21 g

Golden Crab Cakes

Serving Size: 2 crab cakes, Total Servings: 6

1 cup Italian-flavored bread crumbs

3 eggs

1 rib celery, chopped

3 tablespoons light mayonnaise

1-1/2 teaspoons Worcestershire sauce

3 tablespoons shredded part-skim mozzarella cheese

1 teaspoon black pepper

3 cans (6-1/2 ounces each) lump crabmeat, drained

2 tablespoons canola oil

1 In a medium bowl, combine all the ingredients except the crabmeat and the oil; mix well. Fold in the crabmeat, being careful not to break up the crabmeat chunks, then form into 12 equal-sized patties.

2 Heat the oil in a large skillet over medium heat. Add the patties and cook for 3 to 4 minutes per side, or until golden brown. Serve immediately.

Exchanges
1 Starch
2 Very Lean Meat
2 Fat

Calories 250
  Calories from Fat . . 107
Total Fat . . . . 12 g
  Saturated Fat . . . . 2 g
Cholesterol . . . . 166 mg
Sodium . . . . 625 mg
Total Carbohydrate . . 15 g
  Dietary Fiber . . . . 1 g
  Sugars . . . . 1 g
Protein . . . . 19 g

Sesame Scallop Stir-Fry

2 tablespoons sesame oil

2 garlic cloves, minced

1 teaspoon crushed red pepper

1 pound bay scallops

2 tablespoons sesame seeds

1 tablespoon ground ginger

1 head bok choy (Chinese white cabbage, about 3 pounds), trimmed and chopped

1 package (16 ounces) frozen stir-fry vegetables, thawed and drained

1 tablespoon light soy sauce

1 Heat the sesame oil in a wok or large skillet over high heat. Add the garlic, crushed red pepper, and scallops and sauté until the scallops are cooked through. With a slotted spoon, remove the scallops to a bowl and cover to keep warm.

2 Add the sesame seeds and ginger to the wok and cook for 1 to 2 minutes, or until the liquid is absorbed. Add the bok choy and the stir-fry vegetables and stir-fry for 4 to 5 minutes.

3 Return the scallops to the wok and add the soy sauce. Stir-fry for 1 to 2 minutes, or until heated through. Serve immediately.

Exchanges
1 Very Lean Meat
1 Vegetable
1 Fat

Calories 109
  Calories from Fat . . . 45
Total Fat . . . . 5 g
  Saturated Fat . . . . 1 g
Cholesterol . . . . 15 mg
Sodium . . . . 205 mg
Total Carbohydrate . . . 6 g
  Dietary Fiber . . . . 3 g
  Sugars . . . . 3 g
Protein . . . . 9 g

Bimini Shrimp Kabobs

Serving Size: 2 skewers, Total Servings: 4

8 skewers

1 pound medium-sized shrimp (40-count), peeled and deveined with tails left on

Juice of 1 lime

1 tablespoon honey

1/4 teaspoon black pepper

1/4 teaspoon ground ginger

2 fresh peaches, peeled and chopped, or 2 cups canned peaches, drained

1/2 small green bell pepper, finely chopped

1/2 small onion, finely chopped

1. If using wooden skewers, soak in water for 20 minutes. Coat a broiler pan or rimmed baking sheet with nonstick cooking spray.

2. Preheat the broiler. Place 5 shrimp onto each skewer and place on the broiler pan.

3. In a small bowl, combine the lime juice, honey, black pepper, and ginger; mix well. Remove 2 table-spoons of the mixture to a medium bowl and set aside. Brush both sides of the skewered shrimp with the remaining mixture and broil for 4 to 5 minutes, or until pink.

4. Meanwhile, add the remaining ingredients to the reserved mixture; mix well to make a peach salsa. Spread the salsa over 4 serving plates and top each with 2 shrimp skewers. Serve immediately.

Exchanges
1 Carbohydrate
2 Very Lean Meat

Calories 135
  Calories from Fat 9
Total Fat . . . . 1 g
  Saturated Fat . . . . 0 g
Cholesterol . . . . 161 mg
Sodium . . . . 186 mg
Total Carbohydrate . . 14 g
  Dietary Fiber . . . . 2 g
  Sugars . . . . 11 g
Protein . . . . 18 g

"Just a short flight from Fort Lauderdale, Florida, is the tiny fishing island of Bimini. Famous for its fishing grounds, the island also boasts many interesting seafood dishes, like this kabob skewered with shrimp, peaches, and peppers."

Sole Amandine

Serving Size: 1 fillet, Total Servings: 4

4 sole fillets (4 ounces each)

1/2 teaspoon black pepper

2 tablespoons corn oil stick margarine

1/4 cup sliced almonds

1 Preheat the broiler. Coat a broiler pan or rimmed baking sheet with nonstick cooking spray. Sprinkle the fillets with the pepper and place on the pan.

2 Broil for 4 to 6 minutes (without turning), or until the fish flakes easily with a fork.

3 Meanwhile, in a small skillet, melt the margarine over medium-low heat. Add the almonds and cook for 1 to 2 minutes, or until golden, stirring constantly. Spoon the sauce over the fillets and serve immediately.

Did You Know . . .

that some fats are better than others? Nuts such as almonds, which are used in this recipe, contain monounsaturated fats, which are the healthiest ones for us. What fats should we keep to a minimum intake? Saturated fats, which are found most commonly in butter, bacon, and meats.

Exchanges

3 Very Lean Meat
2 Fat

Calories 202
    Calories from Fat . . 100
Total Fat . . . . 11 g
    Saturated Fat . . . . . . 1.4 g
Cholesterol . . . . 60 mg
Sodium . . . . 152 mg
Total Carbohydrate . . . 2 g
    Dietary Fiber . . . . 1 g
    Sugars . . . . 0 g
Protein . . . . 23 g

Seasoned Steamers

Serving Size: 1 dozen clams, Total Servings: 4

1/2 cup water

2 tablespoons corn oil stick margarine

4 garlic cloves, minced

1/4 cup chopped fresh parsley

1/4 teaspoon crushed red pepper

4 dozen littleneck clams, scrubbed

1 In a soup pot, combine the water, margarine, garlic, parsley, and red pepper. Cover and bring to a boil over high heat.

2 Add the clams to the pot. Cover and reduce the heat to medium. Simmer for 6 to 8 minutes, or until all the clams have opened. **Discard any clams that do not open.**

3 Serve the clams with the broth from the pot.

Exchanges
1/2 Carbohydrate
4 Very Lean Meat
1 Fat

Calories	234
Calories from Fat . . .	72
Total Fat	8 g
Saturated Fat	1.3 g
Cholesterol	80 mg
Sodium	195 mg
Total Carbohydrate . . .	7 g
Dietary Fiber	0 g
Sugars	6 g
Protein	31 g

"We don't need to go to the beach to enjoy a clambake. Nope! We can simply prepare this treat from the sea right in our own kitchens. AND BE CAREFUL! Those clam shells get HOT!"

Sesame-Crusted Tuna

Serving Size: 1 tuna steak, Total Servings: 4

4 tuna steaks (4 ounces each)

2 teaspoons sesame oil

1 garlic clove, minced

1/8 teaspoon salt

1/2 teaspoon black pepper

1/2 cup sesame seeds

1 Rub both sides of the tuna steaks with the sesame oil and garlic, then season with the salt and black pepper.

2 Place the sesame seeds in a shallow dish and press the tuna into the seeds to coat completely.

3 Heat a large skillet over medium-high heat. Add the coated fish and cook for 3 to 4 minutes per side, or until desired doneness.

Finishing Touch

If sodium is not a concern for you, drizzle this with light soy sauce just before serving.

Exchanges
4 Lean Meat
1 Fat

Calories 281
 Calories from Fat . . 150
Total Fat . . . . 17 g
 Saturated Fat . . . . 2 g
Cholesterol . . . . 42 mg
Sodium . . . . 114 mg
Total Carbohydrate . . . 4 g
 Dietary Fiber . . . . 2 g
 Sugars . . . . 2 g
Protein . . . . 29 g

Veggie-Lovers' Entrées

Lasagna Primavera

Serving Size: 1/8 recipe, Total Servings: 8

9 lasagna noodles (8 ounces)

2 tablespoons vegetable oil

2 yellow squash, cut into 1/2-inch chunks

1 medium zucchini, cut into 1/2-inch chunks

1 large red bell pepper, chopped

1/2 pound fresh mushrooms, sliced

3 garlic cloves, minced

1 container (15 ounces) fat-free ricotta cheese

2 cups (8 ounces) shredded fat-free mozzarella cheese, divided

1/2 cup freshly grated Parmesan cheese

1 egg

1/2 teaspoon black pepper

1 jar (28 ounces) light spaghetti sauce

Exchanges
1-1/2 Starch
3 Vegetable
2 Very Lean Meat
1 Fat

Calories 322
  Calories from Fat . . . 67
Total Fat . . . . 7 g
  Saturated Fat . . . . . . 1.6 g
Cholesterol . . . . 53 mg
Sodium . . . . 920 mg
Total Carbohydrate . . 39 g
  Dietary Fiber . . . . 5 g
  Sugars . . . . 13 g
Protein . . . . 25 g

1 Preheat the oven to 375°F. Cook lasagna noodles according to package directions, omitting the salt; drain and set aside. Coat a 9" × 13" baking dish with nonstick cooking spray.

2 In a large skillet, heat the oil over medium-high heat. Add the yellow squash, zucchini, bell pepper, mushrooms, and garlic, and sauté for 4 to 5 minutes, or until tender. Remove from the heat and set aside. In a large bowl, combine the ricotta cheese, 1-1/2 cups mozzarella cheese, the Parmesan cheese, egg, and black pepper; mix well.

3 Spread one-third of the spaghetti sauce evenly over the bottom of the baking dish. Place 3 noodles over the sauce, then spread one-third of the cheese mixture over the noodles. Spoon one-third of the vegetable mixture over that. Repeat the layers two more times; top with the remaining 1/2 cup mozzarella cheese.

4 Cover with aluminum foil and bake for 45 minutes. Remove the aluminum foil and bake for 10 to 12 more minutes, or until heated through and the cheese is golden. Allow to sit for 5 to 10 minutes before serving.

Finishing Touch

A fresh garden salad really rounds out this meal. See how awesome it looks in Photo Insert D.

Chunky Veggie Chili

1 tablespoon olive oil

1 large onion, chopped

2 cans (14-1/2 ounces each) diced tomatoes, undrained

2/3 cup hot salsa

1-1/2 teaspoons chili powder

1-1/2 teaspoons ground cumin

2 cans (15 to 16 ounces each) red kidney beans, rinsed and drained

1 large red bell pepper, chopped

1 large zucchini, cut into 1/2-inch chunks

1 medium-sized yellow squash, cut into 1/2-inch chunks

1 In a large saucepan, heat the oil over medium heat. Add the onion and sauté for 2 to 3 minutes.

2 Add the tomatoes, salsa, chili powder, and cumin. Reduce the heat to low, cover, and simmer for 10 minutes.

3 Add the remaining ingredients, cover, and simmer for 20 to 25 minutes, or until the vegetables are tender. Ladle into bowls and serve.

Exchanges
1-1/2 Starch
2 Vegetable

Calories 162
   Calories from Fat . . . 21
Total Fat . . . . 2 g
   Saturated Fat . . . . 0 g
Cholesterol . . . . 0 mg
Sodium . . . . 396 mg
Total Carbohydrate . . 29 g
   Dietary Fiber . . . . 8 g
   Sugars . . . . 9 g
Protein . . . . 9 g

Fresh Mozzarella Pizza

Serving Size: 1 slice, Total Servings: 8

1 refrigerated pizza dough (13-1/2 ounces)

1 tablespoon olive oil

2 garlic cloves, minced

2 ounces fresh mozzarella cheese, shredded (see below)

3 plum tomatoes, thinly sliced

2 tablespoons chopped fresh basil

1 Preheat the oven to 450°F. Using your fingertips or the heel of your hand, spread the dough to cover the bottom of a 12-inch pizza pan, creating a rim at the edges.

2 In a small bowl, combine the olive oil and garlic; mix well and brush over the crust. Top with the cheese and tomato slices. Bake for 10 to 12 minutes, or until the crust is crisp and brown.

3 Remove from the oven and sprinkle with the basil. Slice and serve immediately.

Exchanges
1-1/2 Starch
1 Fat

Calories 159
  Calories from Fat . . . 41
Total Fat . . . . 5 g
  Saturated Fat . . . . . . 1.4 g
Cholesterol . . . . 2 mg
Sodium . . . . 392 mg
Total Carbohydrate . . 25 g
  Dietary Fiber . . . . 1 g
  Sugars . . . . 4 g
Protein . . . . 6 g

"You'll usually find delicate-tasting fresh mozzarella packed in whey or water. And if you're lucky enough to find buffalo mozzarella, made from a combination of water buffalo milk and cow's milk, give it a try. It's the most sought-after type of fresh mozzarella, with a much softer texture than regular mozzarella. Now, THAT'S SOFT!"

Mexican Omelet Cups

Serving Size: 1 cup, Total Servings: 6

1 cup egg substitute

1 can (4-1/2 ounces) chopped green chilies, rinsed and drained

1 can (4 ounces) mushroom stems and pieces, rinsed and drained

1/2 cup (2 ounces) shredded Mexican cheese blend

1 Preheat the oven to 350°F. Coat 6 muffin cups with nonstick cooking spray.

2 In a large bowl, combine all the ingredients; mix well, then spoon into the muffin cups.

3 Bake for 25 to 30 minutes, or until the eggs are set. Serve immediately.

Finishing Touch

Serve this with a little salsa and warm flour tortillas to make it a complete Mexican-style breakfast.

Exchanges
1 Lean Meat

Calories 63
  Calories from Fat . . . 27
Total Fat . . . . 3 g
  Saturated Fat . . . . 2 g
Cholesterol . . . . 8 mg
Sodium . . . . 283 mg
Total Carbohydrate . . . 2 g
  Dietary Fiber . . . . 1 g
  Sugars . . . . 0 g
Protein . . . . 6 g

Spinach Manicotti

1 package (8 ounces) manicotti shells (14 shells)

1 small onion, diced

2 garlic cloves, minced

1/4 pound fresh mushrooms, diced

1 container (32 ounces) fat-free ricotta cheese

1 cup (4 ounces) shredded part-skim mozzarella cheese

1 egg

1 package (10 ounces) frozen spinach, thawed and squeezed dry

1 teaspoon dried basil

1 teaspoon dried oregano

1/2 teaspoon black pepper

2 cups light spaghetti sauce

2 tablespoons freshly grated Parmesan cheese

1 Cook the manicotti shells according to the package directions, omitting the salt; drain, rinse, drain again, and place in a large baking dish. Preheat the oven to 400°F.

2 Coat a small saucepan with nonstick cooking spray. Add the onion and garlic and sauté over medium heat until tender. Add the mushrooms and sauté until brown.

3 Meanwhile, in a large bowl, combine the ricotta and mozzarella cheeses, the egg, spinach, basil, oregano, and pepper. Add the onion mixture; mix well.

4 Spoon the mixture into the manicotti shells (see Note), top with the spaghetti sauce, and sprinkle with the Parmesan cheese. Cover with aluminum foil and bake for 30 to 35 minutes, or until heated through.

Exchanges

3 Carbohydrate
3 Very Lean Meat

Calories 320
Calories from Fat . . . 47
Total Fat . . . . 5 g
Saturated Fat . . . . . . 2.3 g
Cholesterol . . . . 84 mg
Sodium . . . . 608 mg
Total Carbohydrate . . 41 g
Dietary Fiber . . . . 4 g
Sugars . . . . 11 g
Protein . . . . 28 g

Note

An easy way to fill the pasta is to place the cheese mixture in a large resealable plastic storage bag, then snip off a corner. Just squeeze the filling into the manicotti shells, using the storage bag like a pastry bag.

Spaghetti Squash Pie

Serving Size: 1 wedge, Total Servings: 6

1 medium spaghetti squash (about 2 pounds)

2 tablespoons canola oil

2 eggs

1/3 cup plus 2 tablespoons freshly grated Parmesan cheese, divided

1 cup fat-free ricotta cheese

1 garlic clove, minced

1 teaspoon dried basil

1 teaspoon dried oregano

1/4 teaspoon salt

1 cup light spaghetti sauce

1/2 cup (2 ounces) shredded fat-free mozzarella cheese

Exchanges
1 Carbohydrate
2 Lean Meat

Calories 181
Calories from Fat . . . 80
Total Fat . . . . 9 g
Saturated Fat . . . . . . 2.2 g
Cholesterol . . . . 91 mg
Sodium . . . . 540 mg
Total Carbohydrate . . 12 g
Dietary Fiber . . . . 2 g
Sugars . . . . 6 g
Protein . . . . 14 g

1. Place whole squash in soup pot; add 1 inch water. Bring to a boil over medium-high heat, cover, and cook for 25 to 30 minutes, or until tender when pierced with a fork. Remove squash to a cutting board and allow to cool for 15 to 20 minutes.

2. Preheat the oven to 350°F. Coat a 9-inch deep-dish pie plate with nonstick cooking spray.

3. In a large bowl, combine oil, eggs, and 1/3 cup Parmesan; mix well and set aside.

4. Cut slightly cooled squash in half lengthwise. Scoop out seeds and discard. Scrape inside of squash with a fork, shredding into noodle-like strands. Stir squash into egg mixture, then pour into pie plate and form into a crust.

5. In a small bowl, combine ricotta cheese, garlic, basil, oregano, and salt; mix well. Spread evenly over crust, then top with spaghetti sauce.

6. Bake, uncovered, for 25 minutes, then remove from oven and top with shredded mozzarella cheese. Bake for 5 more minutes, or until cheese melts. Remove from oven and sprinkle with remaining 2 tablespoons Parmesan. Let cool for 10 minutes before cutting into wedges and serving.

Pesto Penne

Serving Size: 1/8 recipe, Total Servings: 8

1 pound penne pasta

1 container (7 ounces) prepared pesto sauce

4 large plum tomatoes, chopped

1 Cook the pasta according to the package directions, omitting the salt; drain.

2 Meanwhile, in a large bowl, combine the pesto sauce and tomatoes. Add the hot pasta and toss until well combined. Serve immediately.

Exchanges
3 Carbohydrate
1 Fat

Calories 285
   Calories from Fat . . . 71
Total Fat . . . . 8 g
   Saturated Fat . . . . 1 g
Cholesterol . . . . 1 mg
Sodium . . . . 284 mg
Total Carbohydrate . . 42 g
   Dietary Fiber . . . . 3 g
   Sugars . . . . 3 g
Protein . . . . 10 g

"Pesto is so flavorful that a little bit packs a big taste. Here we can enjoy all those flavors without any guilt!"

Balsamic Veggie Kabobs

Serving Size: 2 skewers, Total Servings: 5

10 10-inch metal or wooden skewers

1/4 cup olive oil

1/4 cup balsamic vinegar

1 teaspoon garlic powder

1/2 teaspoon salt

1/2 teaspoon black pepper

1 medium-sized yellow squash, cut into 20 chunks

1 red onion, cut into 20 chunks

1 medium-sized zucchini, cut into 20 chunks

20 large mushrooms

1 If using wooden skewers, soak them in water for 20 minutes. In a small bowl, combine the oil, vinegar, garlic powder, salt, and pepper; mix well.

2 Alternately thread 2 chunks each of the yellow squash, onion, and zucchini and 2 mushrooms onto each skewer. Place the skewers on a 10" × 15" rimmed baking sheet and pour the oil-and-vinegar marinade over the vegetables. Marinate for 30 minutes, turning after 15 minutes.

3 Preheat the grill to medium-high heat and grill the kabobs for 8 to 10 minutes, or until fork-tender, basting occasionally with the marinade.

Exchanges
2 Vegetable
1 Fat

Calories 100
Calories from Fat . . . 49
Total Fat . . . . 5 g
Saturated Fat . . . . 1 g
Cholesterol . . . . 0 mg
Sodium . . . . 123 mg
Total Carbohydrate . . 12 g
Dietary Fiber . . . . 3 g
Sugars . . . . 7 g
Protein . . . . 3 g

Note

Prefer not to heat up the grill? Just preheat the broiler and broil the kabobs for 12 to 15 minutes, turning and basting halfway through the cooking.

Roasted Pepper Pizza

Serving Size: 1 slice, Total Servings: 8

1 pound frozen bread dough, thawed

2 tablespoons olive oil

1/4 teaspoon garlic powder

1/4 teaspoon onion powder

1/4 teaspoon black pepper

3 medium bell peppers (red, green, and yellow, or any combination), sliced into 1-inch strips

2/3 cup light spaghetti sauce

1 cup (4 ounces) shredded reduced-fat mozzarella cheese

1 Preheat the oven to 450°F. Coat a 12-inch pizza pan with nonstick cooking spray. Using your fingertips or the heel of your hand, spread the dough so that it covers the bottom of the pan.

2 In a small bowl, combine the oil, garlic powder, onion powder, and black pepper. Add the bell peppers and toss to coat, then place in a 9" × 13" baking dish. Bake for 20 to 25 minutes, or until the peppers are fork-tender.

3 Spread the sauce over the dough and sprinkle with the mozzarella cheese.

4 Place the roasted peppers over the cheese and bake for 13 to 15 minutes, or until the crust is crisp and brown. Cut and serve.

Exchanges
2 Starch
1 Vegetable
1-1/2 Fat

Calories 240
  Calories from Fat . . . 69
Total Fat . . . . 8 g
  Saturated Fat . . . . . . 2.3 g
Cholesterol . . . . 8 mg
Sodium . . . . 532 mg
Total Carbohydrate . . 33 g
  Dietary Fiber . . . . 3 g
  Sugars . . . . 5 g
Protein . . . . 10 g

"Why order from the pizzeria when you can make an even healthier pie right in your own kitchen? Let everyone get in on the fun by dividing the dough into individual pieces and having them build their own pizzas. The kids will especially love it!"

Smooth & Creamy Mac 'n' Cheese

Serving Size: 1/6 recipe, Total Servings: 6

1 package (8 ounces) elbow macaroni

2 teaspoons corn oil stick margarine

2 tablespoons all-purpose flour

1/4 teaspoon salt

1/4 teaspoon black pepper

1 can (12 ounces) low-fat evaporated milk

3/4 cup (3 ounces) reduced-fat shredded sharp Cheddar cheese

3/4 cup (3 ounces) fat-free shredded sharp Cheddar cheese

1 Preheat the oven to 375°F. Coat an 8-inch square baking dish with nonstick cooking spray. Cook the macaroni according to package directions, omitting the salt; drain.

2 Meanwhile, in a large saucepan, melt the margarine over high heat; add the flour, salt, and pepper. Slowly whisk in the evaporated milk and continue cooking for 3 to 4 minutes, or until the mixture begins to thicken.

3 Remove the saucepan from the heat and add the macaroni and the cheese; mix well, then pour into the baking dish. Bake for 20 to 22 minutes, or until bubbly and heated through.

Exchanges

2 Starch
1/2 Fat-Free Milk
1 Lean Meat

Calories 264	
Calories from Fat . . . 46	
Total Fat . . . . 5 g	
Saturated Fat . . . . . . 2.1 g	
Cholesterol . . . . 11 mg	
Sodium . . . . 451 mg	
Total Carbohydrate . . 37 g	
Dietary Fiber . . . . 1 g	
Sugars . . . . 8 g	
Protein . . . . 17 g	

"To keep our fat intake down, we can use stronger-flavored cheeses. Because they have stronger flavor, we don't need to use as much as we do of the milder ones."

Roasted Veggie Melt

Serving Size: 1 slice, Total Servings: 6

1 medium eggplant, peeled and cut into 1/4-inch slices

1 medium-sized red onion, cut into 1/2-inch slices

1 medium-sized red bell pepper, cut into 8 strips

1/4 cup olive oil

1/2 teaspoon dried oregano

1/2 teaspoon dried thyme

1/4 teaspoon salt

1/4 teaspoon black pepper

1/2 cup (2 ounces) shredded reduced-fat mozzarella cheese

1 loaf (10 ounces) French bread, split in half lengthwise

1 Preheat the oven to 450°F. In a large roasting pan or rimmed baking sheet, combine all the ingredients except the cheese and bread; toss until well combined. Roast for 35 to 40 minutes, or until the vegetables are tender.

2 Sprinkle with the cheese and bake for 3 to 4 more minutes, or until the cheese melts.

3 Place the roasted vegetables evenly over the cut sides of the French bread, then cut each half into thirds and serve immediately.

Exchanges
1-1/2 Starch
2 Vegetable
2 Fat

Calories 269	
Calories from Fat . . 108	
Total Fat . . . . 12 g	
Saturated Fat . . . . . . 2.4 g	
Cholesterol . . . . 5 mg	
Sodium . . . . 453 mg	
Total Carbohydrate . . 34 g	
Dietary Fiber . . . . 4 g	
Sugars . . . . 4 g	
Protein . . . . 8 g	

"Although this sandwich is at its best served hot, it's really good cold, too. And since it's pretty big, don't worry about not finishing it at one sitting. Remember, eat just enough to feel satisfied ... NOT stuffed."

Caesar Pasta Primavera

1 package (12 ounces) bow-tie pasta

2 tablespoons olive oil

1/4 pound asparagus, cut into 1-1/2-inch pieces

1/4 pound snow peas, trimmed

2 medium carrots, thinly sliced

1 medium-sized yellow or red bell pepper, cut into 1-inch chunks

3 medium plum tomatoes, cut into thin wedges

3 garlic cloves, minced

1 can (14-1/2 ounces) ready-to-use reduced-sodium chicken or vegetable broth

1 package (1.2 ounces) dry Caesar dressing mix

2 tablespoons grated Parmesan cheese (optional)

1 Cook the pasta according to the package directions, omitting the salt; drain. Meanwhile, in a large skillet, heat the olive oil over medium heat and sauté the asparagus, snow peas, carrots, and bell pepper for 2 minutes. Stir in the tomatoes and garlic.

2 In a small bowl, combine the chicken broth and dressing mix; pour over the vegetables and bring to a boil. Reduce the heat to low and simmer for 5 to 7 minutes, or until the vegetables are crisp-tender, stirring occasionally.

3 In a large bowl, combine the hot pasta and the vegetable mixture; add the Parmesan cheese, if desired, and toss until well coated. Serve immediately.

Exchanges
3 Carbohydrate
1 Vegetable
1/2 Fat

Calories 300
  Calories from Fat . . . 47
Total Fat . . . . 5 g
  Saturated Fat . . . . 1 g
Cholesterol . . . . 0 mg
Sodium . . . . 958 mg
Total Carbohydrate . . 53 g
  Dietary Fiber . . . . 4 g
  Sugars . . . . 10 g
Protein . . . . 10 g

Finishing Touch

In place of packaged grated Parmesan cheese, use a vegetable peeler to peel thin slices of fresh Parmesan cheese for topping each serving.

Roasted Vegetable Stack

Serving Size: 1 square, Total Servings: 4

Nonstick cooking spray

1 medium eggplant, cut lengthwise into 6 slices

1 medium zucchini, cut lengthwise into 4 slices

1 large yellow squash, cut lengthwise into 4 slices

1 large red bell pepper, cut into 1/2-inch strips

1/2 teaspoon salt

1/2 teaspoon black pepper

1/2 cup fat-free ricotta cheese

2 tablespoons chopped fresh basil

3/4 cup (3 ounces) finely shredded part-skim mozzarella cheese

1/4 cup tomato sauce

1 Preheat the oven to 425°F. Coat 2 baking sheets with nonstick cooking spray.

2 Place the vegetables on the baking sheets in a single layer. Lightly spray with nonstick cooking spray and season with salt and black pepper on both sides. Bake for 16 to 20 minutes, or until tender.

3 Remove from the oven and reduce the oven temperature to 350°F. Coat an 8-inch square baking dish with nonstick cooking spray. Place 3 slices of the roasted eggplant in the bottom of the baking dish. Spread half the ricotta cheese, half the chopped basil, and 1/4 cup shredded mozzarella cheese over that.

4 Continue to layer with the zucchini slices, yellow squash slices, and strips of red peppers. Spread the remaining half of the ricotta cheese and basil, and 1/4 cup mozzarella cheese on top.

5 Place the remaining 3 slices of eggplant over that and top with the tomato sauce and the remaining 1/4 cup mozzarella cheese. Bake for 10 to 12 minutes, or until heated through and the cheese is melted. Cut into 4 squares and serve.

Exchanges
3 Vegetable
1 Lean Meat

Calories 142	
Calories from Fat . . . 35	
Total Fat . . . . 4 g	
Saturated Fat . . . . . . 2.2 g	
Cholesterol . . . . 24 mg	
Sodium . . . . 547 mg	
Total Carbohydrate . . 18 g	
Dietary Fiber . . . . 5 g	
Sugars . . . . 9 g	
Protein . . . . 12 g	

Confetti Quesadillas

Serving Size: 2 slices, Total Servings: 4

Nonstick cooking spray

1 package (9 ounces) frozen cut asparagus, thawed and well drained

1 medium-sized red onion, finely chopped

1 can (8-3/4 ounces) whole kernel corn, well drained

2/3 cup (2-2/3 ounces) shredded reduced-fat Colby-Jack cheese

1 teaspoon ground cumin

4 8-inch fat-free flour tortillas

1/4 cup fat-free sour cream

2 scallions, sliced

1 Preheat the oven to 450°F. Coat 2 rimmed baking sheets with nonstick cooking spray. In a medium bowl, combine the asparagus, onion, corn, cheese, and cumin; mix well.

2 Place one tortilla on a baking sheet, top with half of the vegetable mixture, then cover with another tortilla; repeat. Lightly coat the tops of the tortillas with nonstick cooking spray.

3 Bake for 6 to 8 minutes, or until the tortillas are crisp and the cheese is melted. Remove from the oven. Cut each quesadilla into quarters and top with sour cream and sliced scallions. Serve immediately.

Exchanges
2 Starch
2 Vegetable
1/2 Fat

Calories 232
Calories from Fat . . . 38
Total Fat . . . . 4 g
Saturated Fat . . . . . . 2.4 g
Cholesterol . . . . 11 mg
Sodium . . . . 556 mg
Total Carbohydrate . . 38 g
Dietary Fiber . . . . 4 g
Sugars . . . . 5 g
Protein . . . . 13 g

"This popular Mexican dish can either be a main dish or an appetizer. And you might want to give it even more zip by topping each slice with a spoonful of Quick-Step Salsa (page 19)."

Great Go-Alongs

# Vegetable Stir-Fry

Serving Size: 1 cup, Total Servings: 8

1 can (15 ounces) baby corn, drained and liquid reserved

2 tablespoons light soy sauce

2 tablespoons cornstarch

1 teaspoon crushed red pepper

1/4 cup peanut oil

4 garlic cloves, minced

1 bunch broccoli, cut into small florets

2 medium bell peppers (1 red and 1 yellow), cut into 1/2-inch strips

1 large onion, cut into wedges

1/2 pound fresh sliced mushrooms

1/2 pound snow peas, trimmed

1 In a small bowl, combine the reserved liquid from the corn, the soy sauce, cornstarch, and crushed red pepper; set aside.

2 In a wok or large skillet, heat the peanut oil over high heat until hot. Add the garlic, broccoli, peppers, onion, and mushrooms. Stir-fry for 6 to 7 minutes, or until the vegetables are crisp-tender.

3 Add the snow peas and baby corn and stir-fry for 3 to 4 minutes, or until the snow peas turn bright green.

4 Add the soy sauce mixture, and stir-fry for 1 to 2 minutes, or until the sauce thickens. Serve immediately.

Exchanges
3 Vegetable
1-1/2 Fat

Calories	138
Calories from Fat	65
Total Fat	7 g
Saturated Fat	1 g
Cholesterol	0 mg
Sodium	290 mg
Total Carbohydrate	16 g
Dietary Fiber	5 g
Sugars	7 g
Protein	5 g

Good for You!

If you change this to suit your own tastes, don't skip the broccoli! Its high fiber count (like those of its cousins, cauliflower and cabbage) means it's a help in lowering cancer risks.

Spiced Sweet Potato Wedges

Serving Size: 10 wedges, Total Servings: 6

5 sweet potatoes
  (about 2-1/2 pounds), peeled

2 egg whites

1/2 teaspoon ground ginger

1/4 teaspoon ground cinnamon

1/8 teaspoon ground nutmeg

1/2 teaspoon salt

1 Preheat the oven to 400°F. Coat 2 large baking sheets with non-stick cooking spray.

2 Slice each potato into 12 wedges.

3 In a large bowl, lightly beat the egg whites, ginger, cinnamon, nutmeg, and salt until foamy. Add the potatoes and toss to coat completely; arrange in a single layer on the baking sheets.

4 Bake for 20 minutes, then turn the potato wedges and bake for 15 to 20 more minutes, or until tender and golden.

Exchanges
2-1/2 Starch

Calories 157
  Calories from Fat 1
Total Fat . . . . 0 g
  Saturated Fat . . . . 0 g
Cholesterol . . . . 0 mg
Sodium . . . . 227 mg
Total Carbohydrate . . 36 g
  Dietary Fiber . . . . 4 g
  Sugars . . . . 17 g
Protein . . . . 4 g

"How sweet (and spicy) it is! It seems like the ginger, cinnamon, and nutmeg we add to the potatoes boost the sweetness that we crave . . . keeping us from having to add any sugar."

Parsleyed Red Potatoes

Serving Size: 3 potatoes, Total Servings: 6

2 quarts water

1 medium onion, quartered

2 pounds (about 18) small red new potatoes, washed

1/4 cup light soft tub margarine

2 garlic cloves, minced

1/4 cup chopped fresh parsley

1 In a soup pot, combine the water and onion and bring to a boil over high heat. Using a potato peeler, peel off a strip of skin from the center of each potato. Place the potatoes in the pot, cover, and cook for 15 to 18 minutes, or until just fork-tender. In a colander, drain the potatoes and onion well; keep warm.

2 Melt the margarine in the same pot over medium heat. Add the garlic and sauté for 1 to 2 minutes, or until tender.

3 Stir in the parsley, then return the potatoes and onion to the pot and toss to coat evenly. Serve immediately.

Exchanges

2 Starch
1/2 Fat

Calories 165
  Calories from Fat . . . 29
Total Fat . . . . 3 g
  Saturated Fat . . . . . . 0.3 g
Cholesterol . . . . 0 mg
Sodium . . . . 68 mg
Total Carbohydrate . . 32 g
  Dietary Fiber . . . . 3 g
  Sugars . . . . 3 g
Protein . . . . 3 g

"A classic side dish, these super spuds are great paired with anything from Caramelized Cola Roast (page 92) to Tarragon Pot Roast (page 93). Try coming up with your own tasty matches!"

Broiled Garden Tomatoes

3/4 cup French-fried onions, crushed

2 tablespoons freshly grated Parmesan cheese

1/2 teaspoon Italian seasoning

3 firm, medium tomatoes, cut in half (see Note)

Fat-free olive oil cooking spray

1 Preheat the broiler. In a small bowl, combine the onion crumbs, Parmesan cheese, and Italian seasoning. Brush the cut side of the tomatoes with the olive oil cooking spray.

2 Sprinkle the tomatoes with the onion-cheese mixture, then place on a broiler pan and broil for about 1 minute, until the tops are lightly browned.

3 Turn off the broiler and close the oven door, leaving the tomatoes inside for 5 to 8 more minutes, or until they are soft but not falling apart.

Exchanges
1 Vegetable
1 Fat

Calories 68
Calories from Fat . . . 39
Total Fat . . . . 4 g
Saturated Fat . . . . . . 1.4 g
Cholesterol . . . . 2 mg
Sodium . . . . 79 mg
Total Carbohydrate . . . 6 g
Dietary Fiber . . . . 1 g
Sugars . . . . 2 g
Protein . . . . 2 g

Note

Cutting a small slice off the bottom of each tomato half before you start will keep them sitting up straight.

Sautéed Green Beans

2 tablespoons olive oil

1/4 cup slivered almonds

1 garlic clove, minced

2 packages (9 ounces each) frozen French-cut green beans

1/4 cup sun-dried tomatoes, chopped

1/4 teaspoon salt (optional)

1/4 teaspoon black pepper

1 In a large skillet, heat the oil over medium heat. Add the almonds and garlic and sauté for 2 to 3 minutes, or until the almonds are light golden.

2 Add the remaining ingredients, cover, and allow the beans to steam for 10 minutes or until tender, stirring occasionally. Serve immediately.

Good for You!

Canola oil and olive oil both earn a "thumbs up" because they contain monounsaturated fat. This fat fights cholesterol buildup by raising HDL (good) cholesterol levels, so look for it in the products you buy. And just because the label on a particular oil or other product claims that it's "light," be aware that that word may simply be referring to its lighter taste.

Exchanges
1 Vegetable
1 Fat

Calories 71
  Calories from Fat . . . 47
Total Fat . . . . 5 g
  Saturated Fat . . . . 1 g
Cholesterol . . . . 0 mg
Sodium . . . . 6 mg
Total Carbohydrate . . . 6 g
  Dietary Fiber . . . . 2 g
  Sugars . . . . 2 g
Protein . . . . 2 g

Pesto Roasted Potatoes

2 pounds small red potatoes, washed and quartered

1/2 cup pesto sauce

1/2 teaspoon black pepper

1 Preheat the oven to 425°F. Coat a rimmed baking sheet with non-stick cooking spray.

2 In a medium bowl, combine all the ingredients and toss to evenly coat the potatoes.

3 Place the potatoes on the baking sheet and bake for 50 to 60 minutes, or until fork-tender. Serve immediately.

Exchanges
2 Starch
1/2 Fat

Calories	177
Calories from Fat . . .	51
Total Fat	6 g
Saturated Fat	1 g
Cholesterol	1 mg
Sodium	244 mg
Total Carbohydrate . .	28 g
Dietary Fiber	4 g
Sugars	3 g
Protein	5 g

"Never made potatoes this way before? Well, by combining them with pesto sauce, they take on a flavor that's so good, you're sure to become known as the Italian kitchen hero!"

Bavarian Cabbage

Serving Size: 1 wedge, Total Servings: 8

1 medium cabbage

1-1/2 cups water

1/2 teaspoon salt

1/4 teaspoon black pepper

3 tablespoons corn oil stick margarine, melted

1/2 teaspoon caraway seeds (see Note)

1 Preheat the oven to 350°F. Cut the cabbage into 8 wedges and place in a 9" × 13" baking dish.

2 Add the water to the dish, season the cabbage with salt and pepper, and cover tightly with aluminum foil. Bake for about 40 minutes, or to desired tenderness.

3 Remove the cabbage to a serving platter. In a small bowl, combine the melted margarine and the caraway seeds; pour over the cabbage and serve.

Note

Try this tasty side dish with New World Sauerbraten (page 94). And if you don't care for the taste of caraway—no problem. Make this a recipe for Garden-Fresh Cabbage by substituting 1-1/2 teaspoons chopped fresh basil for the caraway seeds.

Exchanges
1 Vegetable
1 Fat

Calories 69
Calories from Fat . . . 40
Total Fat . . . . 4 g
Saturated Fat . . . . . . 0.8 g
Cholesterol . . . . 0 mg
Sodium . . . . 211 mg
Total Carbohydrate . . . 7 g
Dietary Fiber . . . . 3 g
Sugars . . . . 5 g
Protein . . . . 2 g

Roasted Vegetables Primavera

Serving Size: 1/6 recipe, Total Servings: 6

1/4 cup olive oil

1 tablespoon chopped fresh dillweed

1 teaspoon salt

1 teaspoon black pepper

1 pound small red potatoes, washed and quartered

3 medium ears corn, husked and cut into 1-inch rounds

1/2 pound baby carrots

1 large red onion, cut into wedges

1/2 pound fresh sugar snap peas

1 Preheat the oven to 400°F. In a large bowl, combine the oil, dill, salt, and pepper.

2 Add the remaining ingredients except the sugar snap peas; toss to coat well, then pour into a 9" × 13" baking dish.

3 Roast, uncovered, for 20 minutes; gently stir in the sugar snap peas, then roast for 25 to 30 more minutes, or until the vegetables are lightly browned and almost tender, turning once. Serve immediately.

Exchanges
1-1/2 Starch
2 Vegetable
1-1/2 Fat

Calories 226
  Calories from Fat . . . 87
Total Fat . . . . 10 g
  Saturated Fat . . . . . . 1.3 g
Cholesterol . . . . 0 mg
Sodium . . . . 426 mg
Total Carbohydrate . . 33 g
  Dietary Fiber . . . . 5 g
  Sugars . . . . 7 g
Protein . . . . 4 g

"Carrots and onions and snap peas, oh my! But it doesn't stop there, 'cause potatoes and corn also jump into the mix to round out this eye-catching dish."

Cheesy Cauliflower

Serving Size: 1/6 recipe, Total Servings: 6

1/2 cup (2 ounces) reduced-fat shredded sharp Cheddar cheese

1/4 cup fat-free mayonnaise

1/2 teaspoon yellow mustard

1/8 teaspoon black pepper

1 package (16 ounces) frozen cauliflower florets, thawed

3 tablespoons French-fried onions

1 Preheat the oven to 400°F. In a medium saucepan, combine the cheese, mayonnaise, mustard, and black pepper over medium-low heat; cook until the cheese is melted, stirring frequently.

2 Add the cauliflower and stir gently until coated. Place in an 8-inch square baking dish and sprinkle with the onions.

3 Bake for 15 to 18 minutes, or until heated through and the onions are golden.

Exchanges
1 Vegetable
1/2 Fat

Calories 60
Calories from Fat . . . 28
Total Fat . . . . 3 g
Saturated Fat . . . . . . 1.4 g
Cholesterol . . . . 7 mg
Sodium . . . . 198 mg
Total Carbohydrate . . . 5 g
Dietary Fiber . . . . 2 g
Sugars . . . . 2 g
Protein . . . . 4 g

"If you're one of those people who turns up your nose at the thought of cauliflower, just give this cheesy version a spin. There's a pretty good chance you'll come away loving it. Would I lie to you?"

Lemon-Roasted Asparagus

Serving Size: 6 to 8 asparagus stalks, Total Servings: 4

2 pounds fresh asparagus, trimmed

1-1/2 tablespoons reduced-fat butter, melted

4 tablespoons fresh lemon juice

4 teaspoons grated lemon peel, divided

1 Preheat the oven to 400°F. Place the asparagus in a 9" × 13" baking dish.

2 In a small bowl, combine the butter, lemon juice, and 2 teaspoons of the lemon peel; mix well and pour over the asparagus. Bake for 20 to 25 minutes, or until desired tenderness (see Note).

3 Remove from the oven and sprinkle with the remaining 2 teaspoons lemon peel. Serve immediately.

Note

Cooking time will vary depending on the thickness of the asparagus. Very thin asparagus will cook much faster than very thick asparagus. And, of course, everybody likes it cooked to a different degree of doneness, so keep an eye on it!

Exchanges
2 Vegetable
1/2 Fat

Calories 64
Calories from Fat . . . 26
Total Fat . . . . 3 g
Saturated Fat . . . . . . 1.3 g
Cholesterol . . . . 6 mg
Sodium . . . . 59 mg
Total Carbohydrate . . . 8 g
Dietary Fiber . . . . 3 g
Sugars . . . . 3 g
Protein . . . . 4 g

Portobello Stuffing

Serving Size: 1/2 cup, Total Servings: 6

2 tablespoons olive oil

1 medium-sized red bell pepper, finely chopped

1 small onion, finely chopped

6 ounces portobello mushrooms, chopped

2 teaspoons rubbed sage

1/4 teaspoon black pepper

1 small corn muffin, crumbled

1 In a large skillet, heat the oil over medium-high heat. Add the bell pepper and onion and sauté for 2 to 3 minutes, or until tender.

2 Stir in the mushrooms, sage, and black pepper, and sauté for 3 to 5 minutes, or until the mushrooms are tender.

3 Stir in the crumbled muffin and cook for 2 to 3 more minutes, or until heated through.

Exchanges
1 Vegetable
1 Fat

Calories	79
Calories from Fat . . .	48
Total Fat	5 g
Saturated Fat	0.6 g
Cholesterol	0 mg
Sodium	27 mg
Total Carbohydrate . . .	7 g
Dietary Fiber	1 g
Sugars	3 g
Protein	2 g

"What can't you do with this versatile superstar of mushrooms? Teaming it with bell pepper, onion, sage, and a healthy corn muffin gets you this incredible stuffing with its meaty taste."

Summer Baked Vegetables

Serving Size: 1/6 recipe, Total Servings: 6

2 tablespoons canola oil

4 tablespoons grated Parmesan cheese, divided

1/4 teaspoon garlic powder

1/4 teaspoon black pepper

2 medium potatoes, thinly sliced into rounds

1 large zucchini, thinly sliced into rounds

2 medium-sized yellow squash, thinly sliced into rounds

4 plum tomatoes, thinly sliced into rounds

Salt to taste

1 Preheat the oven to 400°F. Coat a 9" × 13" baking dish with nonstick cooking spray.

2 In a large bowl, combine the oil, 2 tablespoons Parmesan cheese, the garlic powder, and pepper; mix well. Add the potatoes, zucchini, and yellow squash, mixing until evenly coated; pour into the baking dish.

3 Place the tomatoes on top and sprinkle with the remaining 2 tablespoons Parmesan cheese. Bake for 30 to 40 minutes, or until the potatoes are fork-tender. Serve immediately.

Exchanges

1/2 Starch
1 Vegetable
1-1/2 Fat

Calories 129
Calories from Fat . . . 58
Total Fat . . . . 6 g
Saturated Fat . . . . 1 g
Cholesterol . . . . 5 mg
Sodium . . . . 94 mg
Total Carbohydrate . . 15 g
Dietary Fiber . . . . 3 g
Sugars . . . . 4 g
Protein . . . . 5 g

"We're really fortunate that today's supermarkets are always stocked with fresh veggies—no matter what season it is!"

Creamy Peas and Onions

Serving Size: 1/2 cup, Total Servings: 4

1 tablespoon canola oil

1 tablespoon all-purpose flour

1-1/2 teaspoons butter

1/4 teaspoon ground nutmeg

1/4 teaspoon black pepper

1 cup fat-free milk

1 package (16 ounces) frozen peas and onions, thawed

1 In a medium saucepan, heat the oil over medium-high heat. Add the flour, butter, nutmeg, and pepper; whisk until smooth.

2 Slowly add the milk, whisking until smooth and thickened. Stir in the peas and onions, and cook for 3 to 4 minutes, until heated through. Serve immediately.

Exchanges
1 Starch
1 Fat

Calories	112
Calories from Fat	46
Total Fat	5 g
Saturated Fat	1.3 g
Cholesterol	5 mg
Sodium	71 mg
Total Carbohydrate	12 g
Dietary Fiber	2 g
Sugars	8 g
Protein	5 g

"Sure, we can buy a pre-made dish like this in the supermarket frozen food section, but look at that nutrition label! We're much better off making it at home. And things always taste better coming from our own kitchens!"

Garlic Mashed Potatoes

6 medium-sized red potatoes (about 2 pounds), scrubbed and cut into large chunks

8 garlic cloves, peeled

1/3 cup fat-free sour cream

1 tablespoon butter

Salt to taste

1/4 teaspoon black pepper

1 Place the potatoes and garlic in a soup pot and add enough water to cover. Bring to a boil over high heat. Reduce the heat to medium and cook for 20 to 25 minutes, or until the potatoes are fork-tender; drain and place in a large bowl.

2 Mash the potatoes and garlic along with the remaining ingredients, until smooth and well blended. Serve immediately.

Exchanges
2 Starch

Calories 159
Calories from Fat . . . 19
Total Fat . . . . 2 g
Saturated Fat . . . . . . 1.2 g
Cholesterol . . . . 6 mg
Sodium . . . . 27 mg
Total Carbohydrate . . 31 g
Dietary Fiber . . . . 3 g
Sugars . . . . 3 g
Protein . . . . 4 g

Apple-Stuffed Acorn Squash

Serving Size: 1/6 squash, Total Servings: 6

1 acorn squash (1 pound), cut in half lengthwise and seeded

1/2 cup unsweetened applesauce

2 tablespoons corn oil stick margarine, melted

1/2 teaspoon ground cinnamon

1/4 teaspoon salt

1 Preheat the oven to 400°F. Place the squash halves cut side up on a rimmed baking sheet.

2 In a medium bowl, combine the remaining ingredients; mix well. Distribute the mixture evenly in the squash halves.

3 Bake for 1 to 1-1/4 hours, or until tender. Cut each squash half lengthwise into thirds, and serve.

Good for You!

Have you had your pectin today? Apples are full of the stuff! Pectin is a soluble fiber, which can lower blood cholesterol levels.

Exchanges
1/2 Starch
1/2 Fat

Calories 62
   Calories from Fat . . . 37
Total Fat . . . . 4 g
   Saturated Fat . . . . . . 0.8 g
Cholesterol . . . . 0 mg
Sodium . . . . 136 mg
Total Carbohydrate . . . 7 g
   Dietary Fiber . . . . 2 g
   Sugars . . . . 3 g
Protein . . . . 1 g

Herb-Roasted Corn on the Cob

Serving Size: 1 ear, Total Servings: 4

2 tablespoons corn oil stick margarine, melted

1 garlic clove, minced

1 scallion, finely chopped

1 teaspoon chopped fresh dillweed

1/8 teaspoon black pepper

4 medium ears fresh corn on the cob, husked

1 Preheat the oven to 425°F. In a small bowl, combine the margarine, garlic, scallion, dill, and black pepper; mix well.

2 Place each ear of corn in a separate piece of aluminum foil and brush with the butter mixture. Wrap each and seal completely, then place on a rimmed baking sheet.

3 Roast the corn for 20 to 25 minutes, or until the kernels are tender. Carefully open the foil and remove the corn. Serve immediately.

Exchanges
1-1/2 Starch
1/2 Fat

Calories 137
   Calories from Fat . . . 57
Total Fat . . . . 6 g
   Saturated Fat . . . . . . 1.2 g
Cholesterol . . . . 0 mg
Sodium . . . . 62 mg
Total Carbohydrate . . 21 g
   Dietary Fiber . . . . 3 g
   Sugars . . . . 2 g
Protein . . . . 3 g

"No matter if you roast it in the oven or on the grill, here's a new way to jazz up an old favorite while adding fiber to your diet. One taste and you'll never put plain butter on your ears again."

Honey-Glazed Carrots

Serving Size: 1/2 cup, Total Servings: 4

1 pound baby carrots

2 tablespoons light soft tub margarine

2 tablespoons honey

1/2 teaspoon lemon juice

1/2 teaspoon ground ginger

1/4 teaspoon salt

1 Place the carrots in a medium saucepan. Add enough water to cover and bring to a boil over high heat. Reduce the heat to medium-high, cover, and cook for 15 to 20 minutes, or until desired tenderness; drain well and set aside.

2 In the saucepan, melt the margarine over medium heat. Add the remaining ingredients; mix well.

3 Return the carrots to the saucepan and toss until mixed well and heated through. Serve immediately.

Exchanges
1/2 Carbohydrate
2 Vegetable
1/2 Fat

Calories 99
    Calories from Fat . . . 23
Total Fat . . . . 3 g
    Saturated Fat . . . . . . 0.2 g
Cholesterol . . . . 0 mg
Sodium . . . . 269 mg
Total Carbohydrate . . 20 g
    Dietary Fiber . . . . 3 g
    Sugars . . . . 14 g
Protein . . . . 1 g

Veggie Couscous

Serving Size: 3/4 cup, Total Servings: 8

1 tablespoon olive oil

1 medium onion, chopped

1 can (14-1/2 ounces) ready-to-use chicken broth (see below)

1 package (10 ounces) frozen mixed vegetables, thawed

1 medium tomato, chopped

1 tablespoon chopped fresh dillweed

1/2 teaspoon ground cumin

1 garlic clove, minced

1 package (10 ounces) couscous

1 Heat the olive oil in a soup pot over medium-high heat. Add the onion and cook for 5 to 6 minutes, or until golden.

2 Stir in the chicken broth, mixed vegetables, tomato, dill, cumin, and garlic; bring to a boil. Boil for 2 minutes, stirring occasionally.

3 Stir in the couscous, cover, and remove from the heat. Let the couscous stand for 5 minutes, then fluff with a fork and serve.

Exchanges
2 Starch
1 Vegetable

Calories 197	
Calories from Fat . . . 18	
Total Fat . . . . 2 g	
Saturated Fat . . . . 0 g	
Cholesterol . . . . 0 mg	
Sodium . . . . 160 mg	
Total Carbohydrate . . 38 g	
Dietary Fiber . . . . 4 g	
Sugars . . . . 5 g	
Protein . . . . 7 g	

"Have you seen the wide variety of packaged couscous in the supermarket rice aisle and wondered how to make your own version? Here's your chance to try this pasta cousin. And after making it this way, you might want to substitute low-fat beef or vegetable broth for the chicken, and maybe even add more fresh dill to boost the flavor. Make it your own!"

Great Go-Alongs

Chunky Pear and Apple Sauce

Serving Size: 1/2 cup, Total Servings: 6

4 medium pears, cored, peeled and cut into chunks

4 medium apples, cored, peeled, and cut into chunks

3/4 cup unsweetened apple juice

1 cinnamon stick

1 In a large saucepan, bring all the ingredients to a boil over high heat.

2 Reduce the heat to low, cover, and simmer for 45 to 50 minutes, or until the desired consistency, stirring occasionally.

3 Serve warm or allow to cool, then cover and chill until ready to serve.

Note

Use your favorite type of apples and pears. I like to use Red Delicious apples and Bartlett pears, but most any types you have on hand can be used. Also, if you prefer your sauce a bit sweeter, add 1 tablespoon light brown sugar to the saucepan with the other ingredients.

Exchanges
2 Fruit

Calories 113
   Calories from Fat 6
Total Fat . . . . 1 g
   Saturated Fat . . . . 0 g
Cholesterol . . . . 0 mg
Sodium . . . . 1 mg
Total Carbohydrate . . 29 g
   Dietary Fiber . . . . 4 g
   Sugars . . . . 25 g
Protein . . . . 0 g

"I love this sauce as a cold snack, but I've even had it served warm as a dessert with a spoonful of vanilla ice cream or low-fat yogurt. Okay, I'll quote Mr. Food again . . . MODERATION IS KEY!"

Sautéed Spinach and Chickpeas

Serving Size: 1/2 cup, Total Servings: 6

1 tablespoon canola oil

1 medium onion, chopped

1 package (10 ounces) frozen chopped spinach, thawed and squeezed dry

1 can (8 ounces) tomato sauce

2 cups water

1 can (15 ounces) chickpeas (garbanzo beans), rinsed and drained

1/4 teaspoon salt

1/2 teaspoon black pepper

1 In a large skillet, heat the oil over medium-high heat. Add the onion and sauté for 2 to 3 minutes, or until tender. Add the spinach and sauté for an additional 2 minutes.

2 Reduce the heat to medium-low, stir in the remaining ingredients, and cook, half-covered, for 20 to 25 minutes, or until the sauce thickens. Serve immediately.

Exchanges
1 Starch
1 Vegetable
1/2 Fat

Calories 132
  Calories from Fat . . . 34
Total Fat . . . . 4 g
  Saturated Fat . . . . 0 g
Cholesterol . . . . 0 mg
Sodium . . . . 427 mg
Total Carbohydrate . . 20 g
  Dietary Fiber . . . . 6 g
  Sugars . . . . 6 g
Protein . . . . 6 g

Did You Know . . .

that spinach is full of iron and vitamins A and C? Now that's good news!

Dazzling Desserts

Nicole's Cherry Bonbons

Serving Size: 1 cookie, Total Servings: 24

3 tablespoons butter, softened

5 tablespoons corn oil stick margarine, softened

1 cup plus 2 tablespoons confectioners' sugar, divided

1-1/2 cups all-purpose flour

2 tablespoons fat-free (skim) milk

1 teaspoon vanilla extract

1/8 teaspoon salt

24 maraschino cherries, drained with 2 teaspoons liquid reserved

1 Preheat the oven to 350°F. In a medium bowl, beat the butter, margarine, and 3/4 cup confectioners' sugar until creamy. Stir in the flour, milk, vanilla, and salt; mix well.

2 Shape into 24 balls. Press each ball around a cherry and place on an ungreased baking sheet. Bake for 18 to 20 minutes, or until light golden. Cool on a wire rack.

3 Place 2 tablespoons confectioners' sugar in a shallow dish and roll the bonbons until lightly coated.

4 In a small bowl, combine the remaining 1/4 cup confectioners' sugar and the 2 teaspoons reserved cherry liquid; mix well. Place in a resealable plastic storage bag. Cut a small corner off the bag and drizzle the glaze over the bonbons.

5 Allow the bonbons to cool until the glaze is firm, then serve, or store in an airtight container until ready to serve.

Exchanges
1 Carbohydrate
1/2 Fat

Calories 95
Calories from Fat . . . 34
Total Fat . . . . 4 g
Saturated Fat . . . . . . 1.3 g
Cholesterol . . . . 4 mg
Sodium . . . . 47 mg
Total Carbohydrate . . 14 g
Dietary Fiber . . . . 0 g
Sugars . . . . 7 g
Protein . . . . 1 g

"Yes, you can have sweet treats, like my favorite bonbons, as long as you properly count your carbohydrates. And don't forget, one gram of carbohydrate has four calories."

Strawberry Charlotte

Serving Size: 1/8 recipe, Total Servings: 8

1 package (4-serving size) sugar-free cook-and-serve vanilla pudding mix

2 cups fat-free (skim) milk

1 quart fresh strawberries

2 tablespoons sugar

3 teaspoons vanilla extract, divided

1 package (3 ounces) ladyfingers, split in half

1-1/2 cups frozen fat-free whipped topping, thawed

2 tablespoons toasted sliced almonds (see Note)

1 Prepare the pudding according to the package directions, using the fat-free milk; set aside to cool.

2 Meanwhile, set aside 8 small strawberries for garnish; chill until serving time. Hull and slice the remaining strawberries and, in a medium bowl, combine with the sugar and 1 teaspoon of the vanilla; set aside.

3 Arrange the ladyfingers in the bottom and up the sides of a 2-1/2-quart glass serving bowl. Pour the sliced strawberries over the ladyfingers. Stir the remaining 2 teaspoons vanilla into the pudding and pour the pudding over the strawberries.

4 Spread the whipped topping over the pudding. Cover and chill for at least 2 hours before serving. Just before serving, garnish with the reserved whole strawberries and the toasted almonds.

Exchanges
2 Carbohydrate

Calories 152
  Calories from Fat . . . 18
Total Fat . . . . 2 g
  Saturated Fat . . . . . . 0.3 g
Cholesterol . . . . 12 mg
Sodium . . . . 104 mg
Total Carbohydrate . . 29 g
  Dietary Fiber . . . . 2 g
  Sugars . . . . 18 g
Protein . . . . 4 g

Note

To toast sliced almonds, spread them on a baking sheet and bake in a preheated 350°F. oven for 6 to 7 minutes, or until just lightly browned. Oh, check out this beauty on Photo Insert I.

Angel Food Surprise

Serving Size: 1 slice, Total Servings: 12

1 prepared (10 ounces) angel food cake

1 pint fat-free vanilla–raspberry swirl frozen yogurt, softened

1/2 cup frozen light whipped topping, thawed

1/2 cup fresh raspberries

Fresh mint sprigs

1 Place the cake on a serving plate. With a serrated knife, slice the top 1 inch off the cake by slicing it horizontally all the way around; carefully remove the top of the cake and reserve.

2 Cut and scoop out a tunnel in the center of the cake, leaving a 3/4-inch border of cake on the sides and bottom. (Reserve scooped-out cake for another use.)

3 Spoon the frozen yogurt evenly into the tunnel, then replace the cake top. Wrap with plastic wrap and freeze until firm; plan to garnish and serve anytime after 2 hours, or up to 3 days.

4 Before serving, dollop the cake with whipped topping and garnish with raspberries and mint sprigs.

Exchanges
1 Carbohydrate

Calories 86
Calories from Fat 4
Total Fat . . . . 0 g
Saturated Fat . . . . 0 g
Cholesterol . . . . 0 mg
Sodium . . . . 62 mg
Total Carbohydrate . . 18 g
Dietary Fiber . . . . 1 g
Sugars . . . . 13 g
Protein . . . . 3 g

"Boy, this dessert couldn't get any easier! Actually, any type of frozen yogurt can work here, as well as different fruits. Plus, you can make it a few days in advance of a dinner party, so there's one less thing to worry about. Oh, yes, why not save the scooped out angel food cake to dip in some Raspberry Fondue (page 175)?"

Chocolate Spa Cake

Serving Size: 1 square, Total Servings: 24

3/4 cup (4-1/2 ounces) semisweet chocolate chips

3 tablespoons low-fat (1%) milk

2 tablespoons unsalted margarine

1 cup sugar

3 eggs

1 cup whole-wheat flour

1 cup all-purpose flour

2 teaspoons baking soda

2 cups chilled coffee

1 Preheat the oven to 350°F. Coat a 9" × 13" baking dish with nonstick cooking spray. In a small saucepan, melt the chocolate chips in the milk over low heat; set aside.

2 In a large bowl, beat the margarine and sugar until creamy. Add the eggs one at a time, mixing well after each addition. Add the chocolate mixture; mix until thoroughly combined. Add the whole-wheat and all-purpose flours, the baking soda, and coffee; continue beating until well combined.

3 Pour the batter into the baking dish and bake for 22 to 25 minutes, or until a toothpick inserted in the center comes out clean. Allow to cool completely, then cut into squares and serve.

Exchanges
1-1/2 Carbohydrate
1/2 Fat

Calories 114
    Calories from Fat . . . 31
Total Fat . . . . 3 g
    Saturated Fat . . . . . . 1.4 g
Cholesterol . . . . 27 mg
Sodium . . . . 116 mg
Total Carbohydrate . . 20 g
    Dietary Fiber . . . . 1 g
    Sugars . . . . 12 g
Protein . . . . 2 g

"Can the words 'chocolate' and 'spa' be used in the same sentence? Of course they can! And topping each serving with a spoonful of light whipped topping or low-fat yogurt and some fresh strawberries, raspberries, or kiwifruit slices can be, well, the icing on the cake!"

Crustless Cheesecake

Serving Size: 1 square, Total Servings: 12

2 packages (8 ounces each) fat-free cream cheese, softened

1/2 cup plus 1 tablespoon sugar

3 eggs

1 teaspoon vanilla extract, divided

1/2 teaspoon fresh lemon juice, divided

1 cup fat-free sour cream

1 Preheat the oven to 325°F. Coat an 8-inch square baking dish with nonstick cooking spray.

2 In a large bowl, combine the cream cheese and 1/2 cup sugar; beat well. Beat in the eggs one at a time, then beat in 1/2 teaspoon vanilla and 1/4 teaspoon lemon juice until well combined.

3 Spoon the mixture into the baking dish and bake for 40 to 45 minutes, or until golden. Remove from the oven and let cool for 10 minutes. Do not turn off the oven.

4 Meanwhile, in a small bowl, combine the sour cream and the remaining 1 tablespoon sugar, 1/2 teaspoon vanilla, and 1/4 teaspoon lemon juice; mix well. Spread over the top of the cheesecake and bake for 10 minutes.

5 Let the cheesecake cool, then cover and chill for at least 4 hours, or overnight.

Exchanges
1 Carbohydrate
1 Very Lean Meat

Calories 111
  Calories from Fat . . . 11
Total Fat . . . . 1 g
  Saturated Fat . . . . . . 0.4 g
Cholesterol . . . . 59 mg
Sodium . . . . 295 mg
Total Carbohydrate . . 13 g
  Dietary Fiber . . . . 0 g
  Sugars . . . . 12 g
Protein . . . . 8 g

"Didn't think you could indulge in cheesecake? Well, get your fork ready because this one's for you! And if you think it's going to have less flavor since there's no crust . . . uh uh! Only fewer carbs."

"In the Can" Cake

1 cup water

2 tablespoons instant coffee granules

1/2 cup raisins

1 teaspoon baking soda

1 cup sugar

3-1/2 tablespoons butter, softened

1/2 teaspoon vanilla extract

1 egg

1/8 teaspoon ground cinnamon

2 cups whole-wheat flour

1 Preheat the oven to 350°F. Coat two clean 1-pound coffee cans with nonstick cooking spray.

2 In a small saucepan, combine the water, coffee, raisins, and baking soda over medium-high heat. Bring to a boil and cook for 2 minutes, stirring constantly. Remove from the heat and allow to cool.

3 In a medium bowl, cream the sugar and butter. Add the vanilla, egg, and cinnamon. Alternately stir in the flour and the cooled raisin mixture, mixing well.

4 Divide the batter evenly between the two coffee cans. Place both cans on a baking sheet and bake for 50 to 55 minutes, or until a wooden toothpick inserted in the center comes out clean. Let cool for 15 minutes.

5 Remove from the cans by opening the bottoms with a can opener and carefully pushing the cakes out the tops of the cans. Cut into round slices and serve.

Exchanges
1-1/2 Carbohydrate

Calories 113
Calories from Fat . . . 23
Total Fat . . . . 3 g
Saturated Fat . . . . . . 1.4 g
Cholesterol . . . . 16 mg
Sodium . . . . 82 mg
Total Carbohydrate . . 22 g
Dietary Fiber . . . . 2 g
Sugars . . . . 12 g
Protein . . . . 2 g

"How about serving this with reduced-fat cream cheese? Mmm!"

Fruit Cocktail Cake

Serving Size: 1 square, Total Servings: 20

2-1/4 cups all-purpose flour

1 cup packed light brown sugar

1/4 cup (1/2 stick) butter, softened

1 can (15 ounces) light fruit cocktail, drained, with juice reserved

1/2 cup egg substitute

1 teaspoon vanilla extract

2 teaspoons baking soda

1 teaspoon salt

1 Preheat the oven to 350°F. Coat a 9" × 13" baking dish with nonstick cooking spray.

2 In a large bowl, with an electric beater on medium speed, beat the flour, brown sugar, butter, the reserved juice, egg substitute, vanilla, baking soda, and salt for 2 minutes, or until smooth. Stir in the fruit cocktail.

3 Pour into the baking dish and bake for 25 to 30 minutes, or until a wooden toothpick inserted in the center comes out clean. Allow to cool completely, then cut into squares and serve.

Exchanges
1-1/2 Carbohydrate
1/2 Fat

Calories 125
   Calories from Fat . . . 22
Total Fat . . . . 2 g
   Saturated Fat . . . . 1 g
Cholesterol . . . . 6 mg
Sodium . . . . 282 mg
Total Carbohydrate . . 24 g
   Dietary Fiber . . . . 1 g
   Sugars . . . . 13 g
Protein . . . . 2 g

"This is a pretty straightforward recipe, so it's the perfect way to get the kids into the kitchen to stir things up a bit."

Apple Crisp

6 medium apples, cored, peeled and thinly sliced

1/4 cup plus 2 tablespoons all-purpose flour, divided

1 tablespoon sugar

1/2 teaspoon ground cinnamon

1/2 cup quick-cooking rolled oats

3 tablespoons light brown sugar

2 tablespoons reduced-fat margarine

1 Preheat the oven to 400°F. Coat a 9-inch microwave-safe pie plate with nonstick cooking spray.

2 In a large bowl, combine the apples, 2 tablespoons flour, the sugar, and cinnamon; mix well. Spoon into the pie plate and cover with waxed paper. Microwave on high power for 4 to 6 minutes, or until the apples are soft.

3 Meanwhile, in a medium bowl, combine the remaining 1/4 cup flour, the oats, and brown sugar; mix well. With a fork, blend in the margarine until crumbly; sprinkle over the apples. Bake for 20 to 25 minutes, or until golden and bubbly. Serve warm.

Exchanges
2 Carbohydrate

Calories 144
  Calories from Fat . . . 16
Total Fat . . . . 2 g
  Saturated Fat . . . . 0 g
Cholesterol . . . . 0 mg
Sodium . . . . 25 mg
Total Carbohydrate . . 32 g
  Dietary Fiber . . . . 3 g
  Sugars . . . . 19 g
Protein . . . . 2 g

Double Chocolate Brownies

Serving Size: 1 square, Total Servings: 16

- **2/3** cup all-purpose flour
- **2/3** cup sugar
- **1/2** cup unsweetened cocoa
- **1/4** cup (1/2 stick) corn oil stick margarine, melted
- **2** tablespoons water
- **1** teaspoon vanilla extract
- **1/2** teaspoon baking powder
- **1/3** cup egg substitute
- **1/4** cup fat-free hot fudge sauce

1 Preheat the oven to 350°F. Coat an 8-inch square baking dish with nonstick cooking spray.

2 In a large bowl, combine all the ingredients except the fudge sauce; mix well, then spread half the batter in the baking dish. Top with the hot fudge sauce, then spread the remaining batter over the sauce.

3 Bake for 25 to 30 minutes, or until a toothpick inserted in the center comes out clean. Cool completely, then cut into squares and serve.

Exchanges
1 Carbohydrate
1/2 Fat

Calories 100
  Calories from Fat . . . 29
Total Fat . . . . 3 g
  Saturated Fat . . . . . . 0.8 g
Cholesterol . . . . 0 mg
Sodium . . . . 69 mg
Total Carbohydrate . . 17 g
  Dietary Fiber . . . . 1 g
  Sugars . . . . 11 g
Protein . . . . 2 g

"When this recipe came across my desk, I almost fell off my chair! Chocolate brownies in a diabetes cookbook?! We tested them and, not only do they work, but they're well within the guidelines for a diabetic meal plan. But what's my tried-and-true philosophy? Moderation is key!"

Strawberry Shortcake

2-1/2 cups reduced-fat biscuit baking mix

3/4 cup fat-free (skim) milk

1 tablespoon corn oil stick margarine, melted

1 tablespoon sugar

1/4 teaspoon ground cinnamon

1 quart strawberries, hulled and sliced

1-1/2 cups frozen fat-free whipped topping, thawed

1 Preheat the oven to 450°F. In a large bowl, combine the baking mix and milk, stirring until a soft dough forms.

2 Turn the dough onto a work surface dusted with baking mix. Knead the dough 10 times, adding a little more baking mix to stiffen it, if needed. Roll the dough out to a 1/2-inch thickness. Using a 3-inch biscuit cutter, cut out 6 circles. Rework dough and cut out 2 more circles using remaining dough. Place the dough circles on an ungreased cookie sheet.

3 In a small bowl, combine the margarine, sugar, and cinnamon; mix well and brush over the dough circles. Bake for 8 to 10 minutes, or until golden. Remove the biscuits to a wire rack to cool completely.

4 Cut each shortcake horizontally in half and separate; place half of the strawberries, then half of the whipped topping over the biscuit bottoms, then replace the tops. Dollop with the remaining whipped topping and decorate with the remaining strawberries. Serve immediately.

Exchanges
2-1/2 Carbohydrate
1/2 Fat

Calories 207
   Calories from Fat . . . 37
Total Fat . . . . 4 g
   Saturated Fat . . . . . . 0.6 g
Cholesterol . . . . 0 mg
Sodium . . . . 436 mg
Total Carbohydrate . . 39 g
   Dietary Fiber . . . . 3 g
   Sugars . . . . 11 g
Protein . . . . 4 g

Peach Crumble

Serving Size: 1/2 cup, Total Servings: 8

6 peaches, pitted and thinly sliced

3/4 cup packed light brown sugar

1 cup coarsely crushed cinnamon graham crackers

1 Preheat the oven to 375°F. Coat an 8-inch square baking dish with nonstick cooking spray.

2 Combine the peaches and brown sugar in the baking dish.

3 Sprinkle the crust graham cracker over the peaches and bake for 30 to 35 minutes, or until the peaches are hot and bubbly. Serve warm.

Exchanges
2-1/2 Carbohydrate

Calories	165
Calories from Fat . . .	12
Total Fat	1 g
Saturated Fat	0.2 g
Cholesterol	0 mg
Sodium	72 mg
Total Carbohydrate . .	39 g
Dietary Fiber	2 g
Sugars	31 g
Protein	2 g

"I do declare, this southern-grown recipe has summer written all over it. As a finishing touch, serve the still-warm crumble with a scoop of low-fat frozen vanilla yogurt. Lawdy, lawdy, they'll be lining up for seconds!"

Almond Biscotti

Nonstick cooking spray

1 cup all-purpose flour

1/2 cup sugar

1/2 teaspoon baking soda

1/8 teaspoon salt

2 eggs

3/4 teaspoon almond extract

1/2 cup whole blanched almonds

1 Preheat the oven to 350°F. Coat 2 rimmed baking sheets with non-stick cooking spray.

2 In a large bowl, combine all the ingredients except the almonds; mix well with a spoon. Stir in the almonds until well blended. (The dough will be thick and sticky.)

3 Divide the dough into 4 equal parts then shape into 2-inch-wide loaves. Place 2 loaves on each baking sheet 2 inches apart.

4 Bake for 15 minutes. Reduce the oven temperature to 325°F. Remove the loaves from the oven and allow to cool for 15 minutes.

5 Cut each loaf into 8 (1/2-inch) slices. Lay the slices cut-side-down on the baking sheets and bake for 15 more minutes. Turn the slices over and bake for another 15 minutes, or until very crisp.

6 Allow to cool, then store in an airtight container.

Exchanges
1/2 Carbohydrate

Calories 44
  Calories from Fat . . . 13
Total Fat . . . . 1 g
  Saturated Fat . . . . . . 0.2 g
Cholesterol . . . . 13 mg
Sodium . . . . 34 mg
Total Carbohydrate . . . 7 g
  Dietary Fiber . . . . 0 g
  Sugars . . . . 3 g
Protein . . . . 1 g

"These crispy cookies are made for dunking, so enjoy 'em with milk or your favorite hot drink."

Tropical Gelatin Salad

Serving Size: 1/2 cup, Total Servings: 10

2 packages (4-serving size) sugar-free orange gelatin

2 cups boiling water

1 cup ice cubes

1 can (15-1/4 ounces) tropical fruit cocktail, drained

1-3/4 cups frozen light whipped topping, thawed

1 In a large bowl, dissolve the gelatin in the boiling water; add the ice cubes and stir until melted.

2 Add the remaining ingredients; mix until thoroughly combined. Pour into a 4-cup gelatin mold or serving bowl.

3 Cover and chill for at least 3 hours, until set. Unmold, slice, and serve.

Exchanges
1/2 Carbohydrate

Calories 50
 Calories from Fat . . . 13
Total Fat . . . . 1 g
 Saturated Fat . . . . 1 g
Cholesterol . . . . 0 mg
Sodium . . . . 47 mg
Total Carbohydrate . . . 8 g
 Dietary Fiber . . . . 0 g
 Sugars . . . . 5 g
Protein . . . . 1 g

"Want to make a hit with the kids? Here's a fun activity for them (and it tastes great, too): Instead of pouring the mixture into a mold, pour it onto a cookie sheet. After it firms up, let the kids at it with different shaped cookie cutters."

Light 'n' Easy Ambrosia

1 can (20 ounces) pineapple chunks in light syrup, drained

1 jar (6 ounces) maraschino cherries, drained and halved

1 can (11 ounces) mandarin oranges, drained

1 cup (8 ounces) low-fat vanilla yogurt

1/2 cup miniature marshmallows

2 tablespoons sweetened flaked coconut

1 In a large bowl, combine all the ingredients and toss until evenly coated with the yogurt.

2 Cover and chill for at least 1 hour, or until ready to serve.

Note

When blood glucose levels are high, so are the levels of glucose in your saliva. Untreated high blood glucose levels can lead to cavities. So don't forget to brush after every meal . . . and especially after dessert!

Exchanges
1-1/2 Carbohydrate

Calories	98
Calories from Fat	8
Total Fat	1 g
Saturated Fat	1 g
Cholesterol	2 mg
Sodium	26 mg
Total Carbohydrate . .	21 g
Dietary Fiber	1 g
Sugars	19 g
Protein	2 g

Raspberry Fondue

Serving Size: 1/4 cup, Total Servings: 5

1 package (12 ounces) frozen raspberries, thawed

1/4 cup sugar

1 teaspoon chopped fresh mint

1 Place the raspberries in a blender and purée until smooth. Strain the purée into a medium saucepan. Using a wooden spoon, force the purée through the strainer, discarding the seeds.

2 Add the sugar to the purée and heat over medium heat until the sugar is melted and the fondue is bubbly, stirring frequently.

3 Stir in the mint, then transfer to a fondue pot and keep warm, or serve at room temperature.

Exchanges
1 Carbohydrate

Calories 58
   Calories from Fat 1
Total Fat . . . . 0 g
   Saturated Fat . . . . 0 g
Cholesterol . . . . 0 mg
Sodium . . . . 1 mg
Total Carbohydrate . . 15 g
   Dietary Fiber . . . . 0 g
   Sugars . . . . 15 g
Protein . . . . 0 g

"Help! Need a fast dessert that'll really wow your guests? This one's a 'quickie' that'll surely fit the bill. It can be served with fresh strawberries, apple slices, chunks of pound cake, well . . . just about anything you can dip works. Get as creative as you want, without getting carried away."

Spiced Apples

2 cups cranberry juice

1 cup water

1/4 cup sugar

2 tablespoons lemon juice

1 cinnamon stick

6 whole cloves

6 medium Red Delicious apples, peeled

1 In a soup pot, combine the cranberry juice, water, sugar, lemon juice, cinnamon stick, and cloves. Bring the mixture to a boil over high heat. Add the apples and return the liquid to a boil.

2 Reduce the heat to low, cover, and simmer for 25 minutes, or until the apples are tender, turning occasionally. Remove the apples from the poaching syrup and place in a serving dish.

3 Boil the poaching syrup rapidly, uncovered, for 10 minutes, or until the liquid is reduced by about one-third. Pour the syrup over the apples. Reserve the cinnamon stick and cloves for garnishing, or discard them.

4 Allow the apples to cool for about 30 minutes and serve warm, or cover and chill until ready to serve, turning the apples occasionally to coat with the syrup.

Exchanges
2-1/2 Carbohydrate

Calories 152
   Calories from Fat 5
Total Fat . . . . 1 g
   Saturated Fat . . . . 0 g
Cholesterol . . . . 0 mg
Sodium . . . . 3 mg
Total Carbohydrate . . 39 g
   Dietary Fiber . . . . 3 g
   Sugars . . . . 36 g
Protein . . . . 0 g

Banana Cream Pie

Serving Size: 1 slice, Total Servings: 8

1 package (4-serving size) sugar-free cook-and-serve vanilla pudding mix

1 cup fat-free (skim) milk

1 large ripe banana, peeled and sliced

1 9-inch reduced-fat graham cracker pie crust

1 container (8 ounces) frozen fat-free whipped topping, thawed and divided

1 In a medium saucepan, combine the pudding and milk and cook over medium heat until thickened, stirring constantly. Remove from the heat, cover the surface of the pudding with waxed paper, and let cool.

2 Place the banana slices on the bottom of the pie crust. Fold half of the whipped topping into the cooled pudding.

3 Spoon the pudding mixture evenly over the bananas, then spoon the remaining whipped topping over the pudding mixture. Cover and chill for at least 4 hours, or until ready to serve. Serve as is or garnish as desired.

Exchanges
2 Carbohydrate
1/2 Fat

Calories 173
  Calories from Fat . . . 33
Total Fat . . . . 4 g
  Saturated Fat . . . . . . 0.6 g
Cholesterol . . . . 1 mg
Sodium . . . . 183 mg
Total Carbohydrate . . 32 g
  Dietary Fiber . . . . 0 g
  Sugars . . . . 13 g
Protein . . . . 2 g

"Take a peek at Photo Insert H to see how yummy this pie looks! It's so flavorful, it's hard to believe that the whole pie has just one banana in it."

Peanut Butter Cup Pie

Serving Size: 1 slice, Total Servings: 10

1 package (4-serving size) sugar-free instant vanilla pudding mix

1-1/2 cups fat-free (skim) milk

1/3 cup reduced-fat chunky peanut butter

1-1/2 cups frozen fat-free whipped topping, thawed and divided

1 package (1.5 ounces) peanut butter cups, chopped

1 9-inch reduced-fat graham cracker pie crust

1 In a large bowl, using a wire whisk, combine the pudding and milk until thickened. Whisk in the peanut butter and 1 cup whipped topping. Stir in the peanut butter cups.

2 Pour the mixture into the pie crust, then spread the remaining 1/2 cup whipped topping over the pie.

3 Cover and chill for at least 4 hours, or until ready to serve.

Exchanges
1-1/2 Carbohydrate
1-1/2 Fat

Calories 184	
Calories from Fat . . . 64	
Total Fat . . . . 7 g	
Saturated Fat . . . . . . 1.4 g	
Cholesterol . . . . 1 mg	
Sodium . . . . 201 mg	
Total Carbohydrate . . 26 g	
Dietary Fiber . . . . 1 g	
Sugars . . . . 11 g	
Protein . . . . 5 g	

"Is your sweet tooth screaming for something rich and flavorful? Practically everything in here is low in fat, but not low in taste, so go ahead and calm that craving!"

Oatmeal Chocolate Chip Cookies

1-3/4 cups all-purpose flour

1 teaspoon baking soda

1/2 teaspoon salt

1/2 cup packed light brown sugar

1/2 cup granulated sugar

6 tablespoons corn oil stick margarine, softened

1/2 cup unsweetened applesauce

2 egg whites

1 teaspoon vanilla extract

2-1/2 cups quick-cooking or old-fashioned rolled oats

1/4 cup miniature semisweet chocolate chips

1 Preheat the oven to 375°F. Coat baking sheets with nonstick cooking spray.

2 In a small bowl, combine the flour, baking soda, and salt; set aside.

3 In a large bowl, beat the brown and granulated sugars, the margarine, and applesauce until smooth. Beat in the egg whites and vanilla. Gradually beat in the flour mixture until smooth. With a spoon, stir in the oats and chocolate chips.

4 Drop by rounded teaspoonfuls onto the baking sheets 2 to 3 inches apart. Bake for 9 to 11 minutes, or until golden. Cool on the pans for 2 minutes, then remove to a wire rack to cool completely.

Exchanges
2-1/2 Carbohydrate
1/2 Fat

Calories 205
   Calories from Fat . . . 54
Total Fat . . . . 6 g
   Saturated Fat . . . . . . 1.4 g
Cholesterol . . . . 0 mg
Sodium . . . . 205 mg
Total Carbohydrate . . 35 g
   Dietary Fiber . . . . 2 g
   Sugars . . . . 16 g
Protein . . . . 4 g

"Mini chocolate chips are really great for our baking 'cause, with them, the saying is true that 'a little bit goes a long way'!"

Poached Pears with Chocolate Sauce

Serving Size: 1 pear, Total Servings: 4

4 firm Bartlett pears, peeled

4 cups water

1 cinnamon stick

1-1/4 teaspoons vanilla extract, divided

1/4 teaspoon ground nutmeg

1/4 cup sugar

2 tablespoons unsweetened cocoa powder

2 teaspoons cornstarch

3/4 cup fat-free (skim) milk

1 Cut a thin slice off the bottom of each pear and stand the pears in a medium saucepan. Add the water, cinnamon stick, 1 teaspoon vanilla, and the nutmeg. Bring to a boil over high heat. Reduce the heat to low, cover, and simmer for about 30 minutes, or until the pears are tender; drain.

2 Meanwhile, in a small saucepan, combine the sugar, cocoa powder, cornstarch, and the remaining 1/4 teaspoon vanilla. Slowly whisk in the milk until smooth then bring the mixture to a boil over medium-high heat, whisking constantly. Cook for about 2 minutes, or until thickened. Allow to cool slightly.

3 Spoon a tablespoonful of warm chocolate sauce onto each of 4 dessert plates. Place the pears on the sauce and spoon more sauce over each, allowing the chocolate to drip down the sides of the pears. Serve immediately.

Exchanges
2-1/2 Carbohydrate

Calories 156
  Calories from Fat 9
Total Fat . . . . 1 g
  Saturated Fat . . . . 0 g
Cholesterol . . . . 1 mg
Sodium . . . . 24 mg
Total Carbohydrate . . 38 g
  Dietary Fiber . . . . 4 g
  Sugars . . . . 31 g
Protein . . . . 3 g

"I know these sound fancy, but don't get nervous—you can do it, no problem! And talk about presentation! If you're in the mood, get creative by making a swirl on the rim of the plate with the chocolate sauce before drizzling it over the pear. Let the photo on the opposite page inspire you."

Poached Pears with
Chocolate Sauce

F

Fruit Tart

G

Banana Cream Pie

H

Strawberry Charlotte

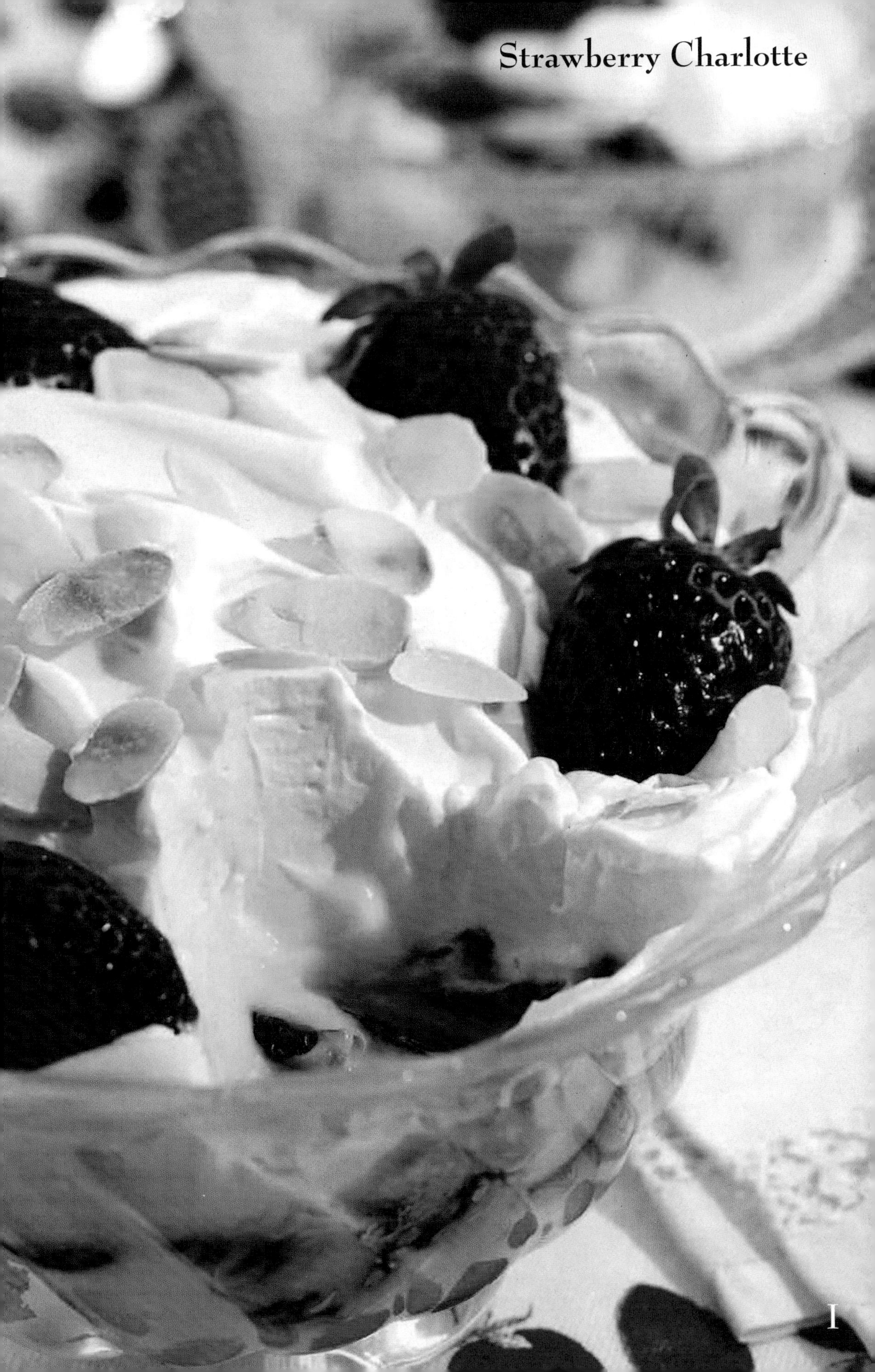

Creamy Chocolate Pie

Creamy Chocolate Pie

Serving Size: 1 wedge, Total Servings: 8

1/4 cup unsweetened cocoa powder

2 tablespoons vegetable oil

1/4 cup sugar

1/3 cup low-fat (1%) milk

4 ounces fat-free cream cheese, softened

1 container (12 ounces) frozen fat-free whipped topping, thawed

1 9-inch reduced-fat graham cracker pie crust

1 In a large bowl, combine the cocoa powder and oil. Add the sugar and milk; mix with a spoon until smooth.

2 Add the cream cheese and beat with an electric mixer on medium speed until smooth. With a spoon, fold in the whipped topping until well blended.

3 Pour into the pie crust, cover loosely, and freeze for at least 4 hours, or until firm.

Finishing Touch

This is good just as is, or you may want to toss on some raspberries, or a dollop of fat-free whipped topping with a few sprinkles. Look how we did it on the opposite page.

Exchanges
2-1/2 Carbohydrate
1 Fat

Calories 241
Calories from Fat . . . 66
Total Fat . . . . 7 g
Saturated Fat . . . . . . 1.0 g
Cholesterol . . . . 2 mg
Sodium . . . . 230 mg
Total Carbohydrate . . 38 g
Dietary Fiber . . . . 1 g
Sugars . . . . 18 g
Protein . . . . 4 g

Fruit Tart

2 cups all-purpose flour

2 tablespoons sugar

1/2 teaspoon salt

2/3 cup canola oil

2 cups plus 2 tablespoons fat-free (skim) milk, divided

1 package (4-serving size) sugar-free instant vanilla pudding mix

1 kiwi, peeled and sliced

1 can (15-1/4 ounces) sliced peaches, drained

1/2 pint fresh blueberries, washed

1 pint fresh strawberries, washed, hulled, and halved

1 Preheat the oven to 400°F. In a large bowl, combine the flour, sugar, and salt; mix well. In a small bowl, whisk together the oil and 2 tablespoons milk; pour into the flour mixture. Using a fork, mix until the dry ingredients are moistened.

2 Using your fingers, press the dough evenly over the bottom and edge of a rimmed 12-inch pizza pan. With a fork, prick the dough all over, then bake for 10 to 12 minutes, or until golden. Remove from the oven and allow to cool.

3 In a medium bowl, whisk together the pudding mix and remaining 2 cups milk until thickened. Spread evenly over the cooled crust.

4 Arrange the fruit in a circular pattern over the pudding, beginning with the kiwi in the center, then continuing with the peaches and blueberries and ending with a border of strawberries. (See Photo Insert G.) Chill for 1 to 2 hours before serving.

Exchanges
1-1/2 Carbohydrate
2 Fat

Calories 188
 Calories from Fat . . . 88
Total Fat . . . . 10 g
 Saturated Fat . . . . 0 g
Cholesterol . . . . 1 mg
Sodium . . . . 174 mg
Total Carbohydrate . . 22 g
 Dietary Fiber . . . . 2 g
 Sugars . . . . 8 g
Protein . . . . 3 g

# Tiramisù

Serving Size: 1 square, Total Servings: 12

1/2 cup warm water

1 tablespoon instant coffee granules

2 packages (4-serving size) sugar-free instant vanilla pudding mix

2 cups fat-free (skim) milk

1 package (8 ounces) fat-free cream cheese, softened

1 package (3 ounces) ladyfingers

1-3/4 cups frozen light whipped topping, thawed

1/2 teaspoon unsweetened cocoa

1 In a small bowl, combine the water and coffee granules; stir to dissolve the coffee. Set aside 1 tablespoon of the mixture.

2 In a large bowl, beat the pudding mix and milk until thickened; stir in the larger part of the coffee mixture. Add the cream cheese and beat until smooth. Split the ladyfingers apart and line the bottom of an 8-inch square glass baking dish with half of them.

3 Drizzle the ladyfingers with the 1 tablespoon reserved coffee mixture. Spoon the pudding mixture evenly over the ladyfingers. Place the remaining ladyfingers on top of the pudding and top with the whipped topping.

4 Sprinkle with the cocoa, then cover and chill for 2 to 4 hours, or until ready to serve.

Exchanges
1 Carbohydrate
1/2 Fat

Calories 105
Calories from Fat . . . 14
Total Fat . . . . 2 g
Saturated Fat . . . . . . 1.3 g
Cholesterol . . . . 11 mg
Sodium . . . . 382 mg
Total Carbohydrate . . 18 g
Dietary Fiber . . . . 0 g
Sugars . . . . 8 g
Protein . . . . 5 g

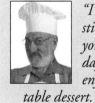
"I know how hard it is to stick to a meal plan, but if you budget throughout the day, you should be able to enjoy a serving of this delectable dessert."

Index

Subject Index

About the American Diabetes Association

The American Diabetes Association is the nation's leading voluntary health organization supporting diabetes research, information, and advocacy. Its mission is to prevent and cure diabetes and to improve the lives of all people affected by diabetes. The American Diabetes Association is the leading publisher of comprehensive diabetes information. Its huge library of practical and authoritative books for people with diabetes covers every aspect of self-care—cooking and nutrition, fitness, weight control, medications, complications, emotional issues, and general self-care.

To order American Diabetes Association books: Call 1-800-232-6733 or log on to *http://store.diabetes.org*

To join the American Diabetes Association: Call 1-800-806-7801 or log on to *www.diabetes.org/membership*

For more information about diabetes or ADA programs and services: Call 1-800-342-2383. E-mail: AskADA@diabetes.org or log on to *www.diabetes.org*

To locate an ADA/NCQA Recognized Provider of quality diabetes care in your area: *www.ncqa.org/dprp*

To find an ADA Recognized Education Program in your area: Call 1-800-342-2383. *www.diabetes.org/for-health-professionals-and-scientists/recognition/edrecognition.jsp*

To join the fight to increase funding for diabetes research, end discrimination, and improve insurance coverage: Call 1-800-342-2383. *www.diabetes.org/advocacy-and-legal-resources/advocacy.jsp*

To find out how you can get involved with the programs in your community: Call 1-800-342-2383. See below for program Web addresses.

- *American Diabetes Month:* educational activities aimed at those diagnosed with diabetes—month of November. *www.diabetes.org/communityprograms-and-localevents/americandiabetesmonth.jsp*
- *American Diabetes Alert:* annual public awareness campaign to find the undiagnosed—held the fourth Tuesday in March. *www.diabetes.org/communityprograms-and-localevents/americandiabetesalert.jsp*
- *American Diabetes Association Latino Initiative:* diabetes awareness program targeted to the Latino community. *www.diabetes.org/communityprograms-and-localevents/latinos.jsp*
- *African American Program:* diabetes awareness program targeted to the African American community. *www.diabetes.org/communityprograms-and-localevents/africanamericans.jsp*
- *Awakening the Spirit: Pathways to Diabetes Prevention & Control:* diabetes awareness program targeted to the Native American community. *www.diabetes.org/communityprograms-and-localevents/nativeamericans.jsp*

To find out about an important research project regarding type 2 diabetes: *www.diabetes.org/diabetes-research/research-home.jsp*

To obtain information on making a planned gift or charitable bequest: Call 1-888-700-7029. *www.wpg.cc/stl/CDA/homepage/1,1006,509,00.html*

To make a donation or memorial contribution: Call 1-800-342-2383. *www.diabetes.org/support-the-cause/make-a-donation.jsp*